MathFlare

Name: ______________________

Class: __________

Teacher: ______________________

Copyright © 2024 MathFlare Publishing.
All rights reserved. This book or any portion thereof may not be reproduced or used in any manner whatsoever without the express written permission of the publisher except for the use of brief quotations in a book review.

Introduction

As parents and educators, we recognize the pivotal role mathematics plays in shaping a child's academic journey and future success. Yet, the path to mathematical proficiency can often seem daunting, fraught with challenges and complexities. That's where the transformative power of MathFlare Workbooks shine through, illuminating the way forward with clarity, precision, and purpose.

Introducing MathFlare Workbooks – a beacon of guidance, a testament to excellence, and a catalyst for achievement. Crafted with meticulous care and expertise, MathFlare Workbooks stand as paragons of educational excellence, designed to nurture young minds, ignite a passion for learning, and develop a deep-rooted understanding of mathematical concepts.

Picture this: your child eagerly delves into the pages of Mathflare Workbook, greeted by a step-by-step guide illuminated with vivid examples that demystify complex mathematical concepts. With each turn of the page, they embark on a journey of discovery, encountering thoughtfully curated practice questions that reinforce learning and hone problem-solving skills. And when they unveil the answers to those very questions, a sense of accomplishment blossoms within them – a tangible reward for their hard work and dedication.

But MathFlare Workbooks are more than just tools for learning; they are pathways to comprehension, fostering a deep-seated understanding of mathematical concepts through a sequential, logical flow. From fundamental principles to advanced problem-solving strategies, every chapter builds upon the last, ensuring a robust foundation upon which future knowledge can be constructed.

As parents, we yearn for nothing more than to see our children thrive, to witness the spark of inspiration ignited within them as they conquer academic challenges with confidence and poise. MathFlare Workbooks serve as partners in this noble endeavor, offering not just practice questions, but the keys to unlocking a world of opportunity.

And for teachers, MathFlare Workbooks stand as invaluable allies in the quest to cultivate mathematical proficiency in the classroom. With answers readily available, instructors can focus on guiding and nurturing their students, confident in the knowledge that MathFlare Workbooks provide a solid framework upon which to build.

In the pages of MathFlare Workbooks, we find not just the promise of academic excellence, but the seeds of a brighter tomorrow. So let us embrace the power of mathematics, let us champion the journey of learning, and let us pave the way for a generation of young minds poised to shape the world. With MathFlare Workbooks as our guide, the possibilities are infinite, and the future, bright.

Table of Contents

MathFlare
MATH WORKBOOK
Grade 2
Step by Step Guide and Essential Practice with Answers
Addition Subtraction
Multiplication
Place Value and Expanded Notations
Geometry
MathFlare Publishing

MathFlare
MATH WORKBOOK
Grade 2-3
Step by Step Guide and Essential Practice with Answers
Addition Subtraction
Multiplication and Division
Place Value and Expanded Notations
Geometry
MathFlare Publishing

MathFlare
MATH WORKBOOK
Grade 3
Step by Step Guide and Essential Practice with Answers
Multiplication and Division
Decimals
Place Value and Expanded Notations
Fractions and Geometry
MathFlare Publishing

MathFlare
MATH WORKBOOK
Grade 1
Step by Step Guide and Essential Practice with Answers
Counting and Numbers
Addition and Subtraction
Place Value and Expanded Notations
Understanding Time
MathFlare Publishing

MathFlare
MATH WORKBOOK
Grade 1-2
Step by Step Guide and Essential Practice with Answers
Counting and Numbers
Addition and Subtraction
Place Value and Expanded Notations
Understanding Time
MathFlare Publishing

MathFlare
MATH WORKBOOK
Grade 3-4
Step by Step Guide and Essential Practice with Answers
Addition Subtraction
Multiplication Division
Place Value and Expanded Notations
Fractions and Geometry
MathFlare Publishing

MathFlare
MATH WORKBOOK
Grade 4
Step by Step Guide and Essential Practice with Answers
Addition Subtraction
Multiplication Division
Place Value and Expanded Notations
Fractions and Geometry
MathFlare Publishing

MathFlare
MATH WORKBOOK
Grade 4-5
Step by Step Guide and Essential Practice with Answers
Multiplication Division
Place Value and Expanded Notations
Fractions and Geometry
Unit Conversion
MathFlare Publishing

Fractions

Fractions represent parts of a whole. They consist of a numerator (the number on top) and a denominator (the number on the bottom).

For example: we have an orange, and we divide it into 5 equal slices. Each slice represents $\frac{1}{5}$ of the orange. Now, if we take 3 of those slices, we have taken $\frac{3}{5}$ of the orange.

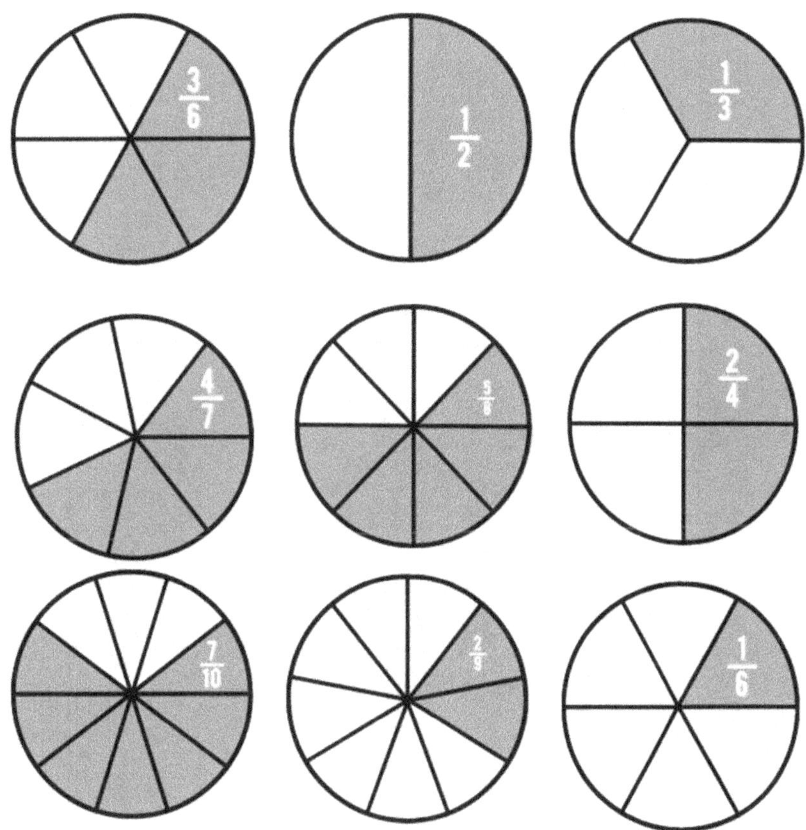

Equivalent Fractions

Equivalent fractions are fractions that represent the same value or part of a whole, even though they may look different.

To find equivalent fractions, you can:

- Multiply or divide both the numerator and denominator by the same nonzero number.
- Simplify fractions to their simplest form.

$\frac{1}{2}$ and $\frac{2}{4}$ are equivalent fractions because if you multiply the numerator and denominator of $\frac{1}{2}$ by 2, you get $\frac{2}{4}$. Similarly, if you divide both the numerator and denominator of $\frac{2}{4}$ by 2, you get $\frac{1}{2}$.

Let's solve a problem:

$$\frac{}{8} = \frac{15}{40}$$

To solve the missing numerator, we can cross multiply.

$$40x = 8 \times 15$$

$$40x = 120$$

$$x = \frac{120}{40} = x = 3$$

$$\frac{3}{8} = \frac{15}{40}$$

Convert Fractions and Decimals

Fraction to Decimal

To transform a fraction into a decimal, we divide the numerator by the denominator.

For instance, $\frac{1}{4}$ equals 0.25 because when we divide 1 by 4, we get 0.25.

In certain cases, the resulting decimal repeats infinitely, like $\frac{1}{3}$, which equals 0.3333...
In such instances, we round the decimal to a specific number of decimal places.

$$\frac{498}{500} = \frac{498 \div 2}{500 \div 2} = \frac{249}{250} = 0.996$$

Decimal to Fraction

Step 1: Write down the decimal as a fraction with the decimal part in the numerator and the place value of the last digit in the denominator.

Step 2: Simplify the fraction if possible.

For example,

$$0.68 = \frac{17}{25}$$

$$\frac{0.68}{1} = \frac{0.68 \times 100}{1 \times 100} = \frac{68}{100} = \frac{68 \div 4}{100 \div 4}$$

Least Common Multiple (LCM)

The Lowest Common Multiple (LCM) of two or more numbers is the smallest multiple that is divisible by each of the numbers.

There are several methods to find the LCM; however, we will focus on only two:

Listing Multiples: List the multiples of each number until you find a common multiple. For example:

$$
\begin{array}{ll}
8 & 8,\ 16,\ 24,\ 32,\ 40,\ 48,\ 56 \\
7 & 7,\ 14,\ 21,\ 28,\ 35,\ 42,\ 49,\ 56
\end{array}
$$

, LCM = $\underline{56}$

Division Method: Divide each number with the smallest prime number that divides at least one of the numbers evenly. The product of all the divisors and quotients is the LCM. For example:

$$
\begin{array}{c|cc}
2 & 7 & 8 \\ \hline
2 & 7 & 4 \\ \hline
2 & 7 & 2 \\ \hline
7 & 7 & 1 \\ \hline
  & 1 & 1
\end{array}
$$

LCM = 2 x 2 x 2 x 7 = $\underline{56}$

Both methods have their advantages. For big numbers, using the division way is usually faster. But if we are working with smaller numbers or like seeing patterns, listing multiples might make more sense.

Mixed Numbers: Mixed into Improper

Mixed numbers and improper fractions are two different ways to represent the same value of a fraction.

1. **Mixed Number:** A mixed number is a combination of a whole number and a proper fraction. For example, $2\frac{1}{3}$ is a mixed number, where 2 is the whole number part and $\frac{1}{3}$ is the fraction part.

2. **Improper Fraction:** An improper fraction is a fraction where the numerator is greater than or equal to the denominator. For example, $\frac{7}{3}$ is an improper fraction because 6 is greater than 3.

To convert a mixed number to an improper fraction, you multiply the whole number by the denominator of the fraction, add the numerator, and then write the result over the original denominator. For example:

$$2\frac{1}{3} = \frac{2 \times 3 + 1}{3} = \frac{7}{3}$$

To convert an improper fraction to a mixed number, we divide the numerator by the denominator. The quotient becomes the whole number part, and the remainder becomes the numerator of the fraction. For example:

$$\frac{7}{3} = 2\frac{1}{3}$$

Let's solve some problems:

$$2\frac{10}{20} = \begin{array}{c} 20 \times 2 = 40 \\ 40 + 10 = 50 \end{array} = \frac{50}{20} = \frac{5}{2}$$

$$\frac{91}{14} = \begin{array}{c} 91 \div 7 = 13 \\ 14 \div 7 = 2 \end{array} = 6\frac{1}{2}$$

$$13 \div 2 = 6 \text{ with a remainder of } 1$$

Mixed Numbers: Addition and Subtraction

To add or subtract mixed numbers, we follow similar steps as when adding or subtracting regular fractions. For instance:

Addition:

- Add the whole numbers: Add the whole number parts of the mixed numbers together.
- Add the fractions: Add the fractions parts of the mixed numbers together.
- Simplify (if needed): If the fraction part of the sum is an improper fraction, simplify it by converting it to a mixed number.

Subtraction:

- Subtract the whole numbers: Subtract the whole number part of the second mixed number from the whole number part of the first mixed number.
- Subtract the fractions: Subtract the fraction part of the second mixed number from the fraction part of the first mixed number.
- Simplify (if needed): If the fraction part of the difference is a negative fraction, borrow from the whole number part or simplify it by converting it to a mixed number.

Let's solve some problems:

$$3\frac{4}{8} + 7\frac{1}{3} = \frac{\frac{4}{8} + \frac{1}{3}}{3 + 7 = 10} = \frac{4\times3 + 8\times1}{8\times3} = \frac{12 + 8}{24} = \frac{20}{24} = 10\frac{5}{6}$$

$$7\frac{4}{6} - 2\frac{3}{8} = \frac{\frac{4}{6} - \frac{3}{8}}{7 - 2 = 5} = \frac{4\times8 - 6\times3}{6\times8} = \frac{32 - 18}{48} = \frac{14}{48} = 5\frac{7}{24}$$

Mixed Numbers: Multiplication and Division

To multiply or divide mixed numbers, we follow these steps:

Multiplication:

- <u>Convert the mixed numbers to improper fractions</u>: Multiply the whole number by the denominator of the fraction, then add the numerator. Write the result over the original denominator.
- <u>Multiply the fractions</u>: Multiply the numerators together to get the new numerator and multiply the denominators together to get the new denominator.
- <u>Simplify (if needed)</u>: If the result is an improper fraction, simplify it by converting it back to a mixed number.

Division:

- <u>Convert the mixed numbers to improper fractions</u>:
- <u>Invert the divisor</u>: Flip the second fraction (the one you're dividing by) so that the division becomes multiplication.
- <u>Multiply the fractions</u>: Multiply the numerators together to get the new numerator and multiply the denominators together to get the new denominator.
- <u>Simplify (if needed)</u>: If the result is an improper fraction, simplify it by converting it back to a mixed number.

Let's solve some problems:

$$1\frac{2}{4} \times 3\frac{1}{6} = \frac{3}{2} \times \frac{19}{6} = \frac{3 \times 19}{2 \times 6} = \frac{57}{12} = 4\frac{3}{4}$$

$$1 \times 4 + 2 = 6 = \frac{6}{2} = \frac{3}{2} \qquad 3 \times 8 + 1 = 19 = \frac{19}{6}$$

$$2\frac{6}{10} \div 6\frac{6}{7} = \frac{\dfrac{13 \times 7}{5 \quad 48}}{\quad} \approx \frac{13 \times 7}{5 \times 48} = \frac{91}{240}$$

$$2 \times 10 + 6 = 26 = \frac{26}{10} \approx \frac{13}{5} \qquad 6 \times 7 + 6 = 48 = \frac{48}{7}$$

Multiplication with whole numbers

To multiply a fraction by a whole number, we simply multiply the numerator of the fraction by the whole number while keeping the denominator the same.

For example, if we have $\frac{2}{3}$ and we want to multiply it by 5:

$$5 \times \frac{2}{3} = \frac{5 \times 2}{3} = \frac{10}{3}$$

Let's solve a problem:

$$1 \times \frac{8}{10} = \frac{1 \times 8}{10} = \frac{8 \div 2}{10 \div 2} = \frac{4}{5}$$

Simplify Fractions

To simplify a fraction means to rewrite it in its simplest form, where the numerator and denominator have no common factors other than 1. We follow these steps:

- **Identify the Greatest Common Divisor (GCD):** Find the largest number that divides both the numerator and the denominator evenly.
- **Divide by the GCD:** Divide both the numerator and denominator by their GCD.

For example, let's simplify. $\frac{12}{18}$

Identify the GCD: The factors of 12 are 1, 2, 3, 4, 6, and 12. The factors of 18 are 1, 2, 3, 6, 9, and 18. The largest number that divides both 12 and 18 evenly is 6. So, the GCD is 6.

Divide by the GCD: Divide both the numerator and denominator by 6.

$$\frac{12}{18} \div \frac{6}{6} = \frac{2}{3}$$

Another way to simplify fractions is to factorize the numerator and denominator completely, and then cancel out common factors. This method is particularly useful when dealing with larger numbers or algebraic fractions.

Multiple Operations Fractions

Fraction multiple operations involve performing multiple arithmetic operations (addition, subtraction, multiplication, division) on fractions.

We follow (PEDMAS that stands for the order of operations in arithmetic) to solve multiple operations Fractions:

1. **Parentheses:** Perform operations inside parentheses first.

2. **Exponents:** Evaluate expressions with exponents or powers.

3. **Multiplication and Division:** Perform multiplication and division from left to right.

4. **Addition and Subtraction:** Perform addition and subtraction from left to right.

For example:

Let's solve the expression: $\frac{3}{4} + \frac{1}{2} \times \frac{2}{3}$

Step 1: Begin by performing the multiplication operation first:

$$= \frac{1 \times 2}{2 \times 4} = \frac{2}{6} = \frac{1}{3}$$

Step 2: Now rewrite the expression with the result of the multiplication:

$$\frac{3}{4} + \frac{1}{3}$$

Step 3: To add fractions, find a common denominator. In this case, the least common multiple (LCM) of 4 and 3 is 12.

Step 4: Rewrite both fractions with the common denominator:

$$\frac{9}{12} + \frac{4}{12}$$

Step 5: Add the numerators together and keep the common denominator:

$$\frac{13}{12} = 1\frac{1}{12}$$

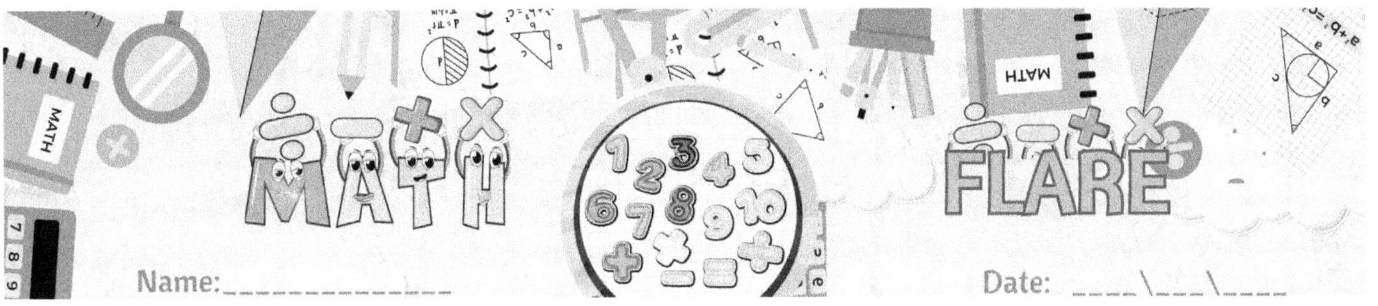

Convert Fractions and Decimals

Convert Fractions to Decimals and Decimals to Fractions.

1. $0.45 =$ _______________

2. $\dfrac{8}{10} =$ _______________

3. $\dfrac{31}{70} =$ _______________

4. $0.667 =$ _______________

5. $0.825 =$ _______________

6. $\dfrac{5}{15} =$ _______________

7. $\dfrac{12}{25} =$ _______________

8. $\dfrac{10}{11} =$ _______________

9. $0.611 =$ _______________

10. $0.333 =$ _______________

11. $\dfrac{4}{5} =$ _______________

12. $\dfrac{5}{6} =$ _______________

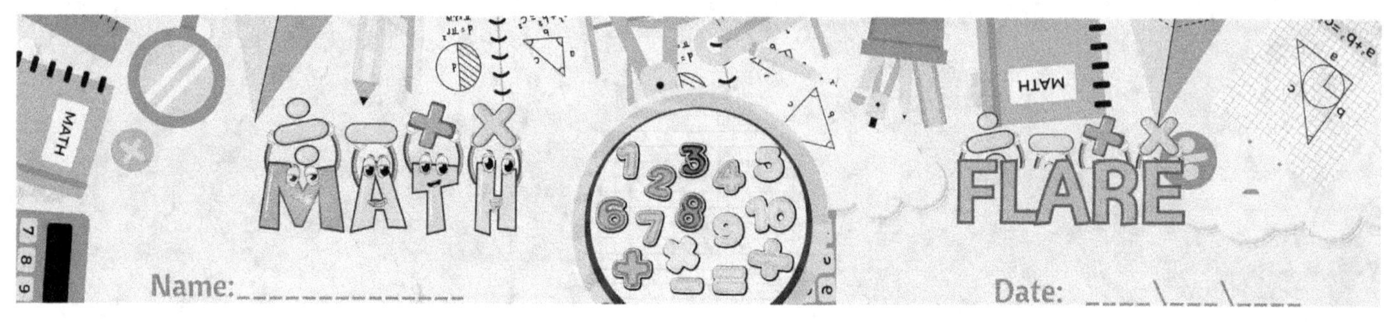

13. $\dfrac{20}{60}$ = ________________

14. 0.562 = ________________

15. 0.948 = ________________

16. 0.5 = ________________

17. 0.233 = ________________

18. 0.692 = ________________

19. $\dfrac{7}{21}$ = ________________

20. $\dfrac{66}{70}$ = ________________

21. 0.4 = ________________

22. 0.094 = ________________

23. $\dfrac{1}{15}$ = ________________

24. 0.52 = ________________

25. $\dfrac{55}{60}$ = _______________________

26. $\dfrac{21}{23}$ = _______________________

27. 0.368 = _______________________

28. $\dfrac{470}{500}$ = _______________________

29. 0.88 = _______________________

30. $\dfrac{4}{8}$ = _______________________

31. $\dfrac{11}{14}$ = _______________________

32. 0.25 = _______________________

33. 0.364 = _______________________

34. 0.833 = _______________________

35. 0.944 = _______________________

36. $\dfrac{4}{9}$ = _______________________

37. $0.627 =$ _______________

38. $\dfrac{22}{40} =$ _______________

39. $\dfrac{3}{5} =$ _______________

40. $\dfrac{6}{16} =$ _______________

41. $\dfrac{2}{36} =$ _______________

42. $0.6 =$ _______________

43. $0.857 =$ _______________

44. $0.05 =$ _______________

45. $0.333 =$ _______________

46. $\dfrac{9}{17} =$ _______________

47. $\dfrac{4}{12} =$ _______________

48. $\dfrac{8}{13} =$ _______________

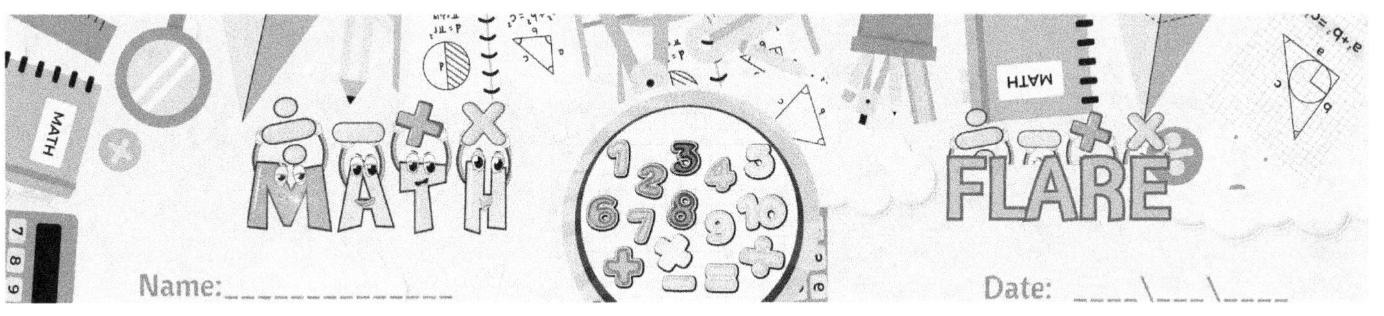

Mixed Numbers: Improper Fractions

49. $3 \frac{9}{12} =$ ______________________

50. $\frac{253}{38} =$ ______________________

51. $\frac{195}{20} =$ ______________________

52. $4 \frac{4}{16} =$ ______________________

53. $9 \frac{7}{18} =$ ______________________

54. $2 \frac{7}{12} =$ ______________________

55. $7 \frac{1}{20} =$ ______________________

56. $7 \frac{2}{4} =$ ______________________

57. $\frac{25}{4} =$ ______________________

58. $5 \frac{6}{17} =$ ______________________

59. $\frac{16}{11} =$ ______________________

60. $1 \frac{18}{38} =$ ______________________

61. $7 \frac{1}{18} =$ ______________________

62. $6 \frac{1}{16} =$ ______________________

63. $9 \frac{5}{10} =$ _______________

64. $4 \frac{7}{8} =$ _______________

65. $1 \frac{2}{5} =$ _______________

66. $5 \frac{3}{11} =$ _______________

67. $\frac{21}{19} =$ _______________

68. $\frac{80}{15} =$ _______________

69. $9 \frac{3}{14} =$ _______________

70. $\frac{38}{4} =$ _______________

71. $\frac{228}{28} =$ _______________

72. $\frac{231}{26} =$ _______________

73. $5 \frac{21}{22} =$ _______________

74. $6 \frac{18}{20} =$ _______________

75. $\frac{85}{16} =$ _______________

76. $\frac{234}{40} =$ _______________

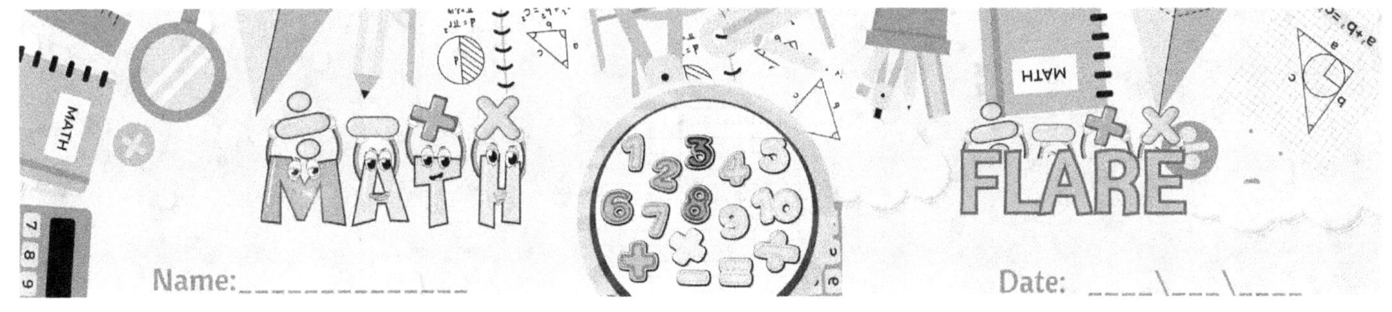

77. $\dfrac{129}{18} =$ _______________

78. $\dfrac{79}{8} =$ _______________

79. $2\dfrac{4}{13} =$ _______________

80. $\dfrac{41}{12} =$ _______________

81. $1\dfrac{1}{4} =$ _______________

82. $\dfrac{240}{38} =$ _______________

83. $5\dfrac{5}{11} =$ _______________

84. $3\dfrac{8}{14} =$ _______________

85. $6\dfrac{4}{20} =$ _______________

86. $4\dfrac{14}{16} =$ _______________

87. $\dfrac{55}{10} =$ _______________

88. $7\dfrac{4}{6} =$ _______________

89. $2\dfrac{23}{32} =$ _______________

90. $\dfrac{85}{14} =$ _______________

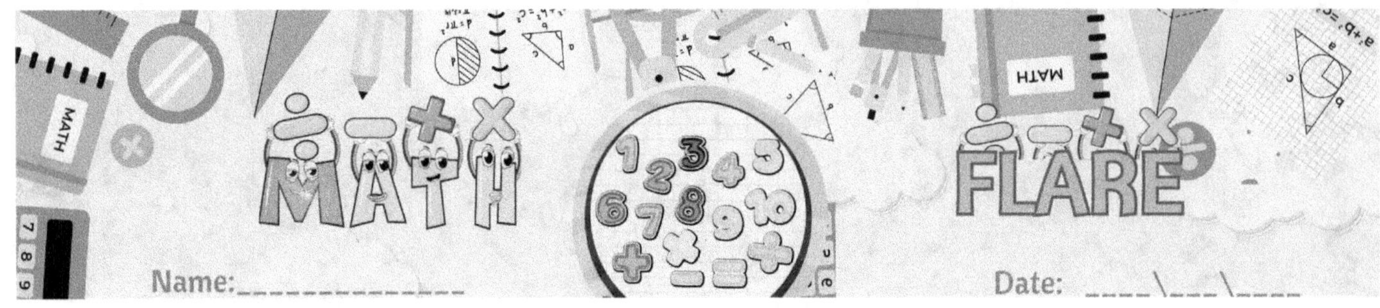

Mixed Numbers: Addition and Subtraction

Calculate.

91. $4\frac{4}{7} - 4\frac{3}{10} =$ ___________________________

92. $5\frac{7}{8} + 3\frac{1}{8} =$ ___________________________

93. $2\frac{2}{8} + 7\frac{3}{10} =$ ___________________________

94. $4\frac{5}{7} + 4\frac{2}{3} =$ ___________________________

95. $7\frac{2}{4} + 9\frac{4}{5} =$ ___________________________

96. $1\frac{6}{9} + 8\frac{1}{6} =$ ___________________________

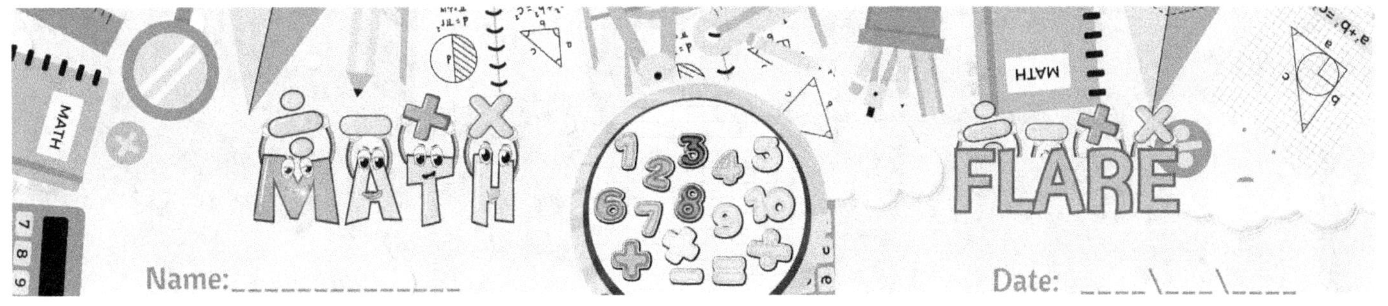

97. $6\frac{1}{2} + 3\frac{4}{6} =$ ___________________

98. $4\frac{2}{10} - 3\frac{4}{7} =$ ___________________

99. $4\frac{1}{2} + 4\frac{2}{8} =$ ___________________

100. $3\frac{2}{9} + 1\frac{2}{3} =$ ___________________

101. $8\frac{3}{5} - 6\frac{1}{4} =$ ___________________

102. $5\frac{3}{8} - 2\frac{6}{7} =$ ___________________

Name: _________________   Date: ____________

103. $6 \frac{2}{9} + 3 \frac{4}{5} =$ _______________________

104. $4 \frac{5}{6} + 1 \frac{1}{2} =$ _______________________

105. $4 \frac{2}{3} + 4 \frac{1}{4} =$ _______________________

106. $1 \frac{8}{10} + 3 \frac{6}{7} =$ _______________________

107. $5 \frac{7}{8} + 6 \frac{1}{4} =$ _______________________

108. $6 \frac{5}{9} - 1 \frac{7}{10} =$ _______________________

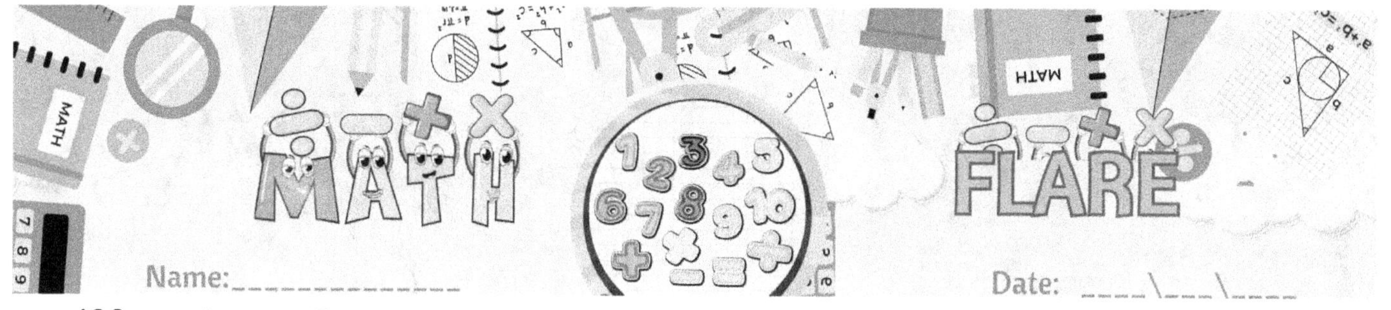

109. $7\frac{1}{3} + 7\frac{3}{6} =$ _______________

110. $3\frac{1}{2} + 5\frac{1}{5} =$ _______________

111. $8\frac{1}{6} - 7\frac{1}{4} =$ _______________

112. $1\frac{2}{5} + 4\frac{3}{9} =$ _______________

113. $8\frac{1}{2} - 5\frac{1}{3} =$ _______________

114. $9\frac{3}{8} + 9\frac{5}{7} =$ _______________

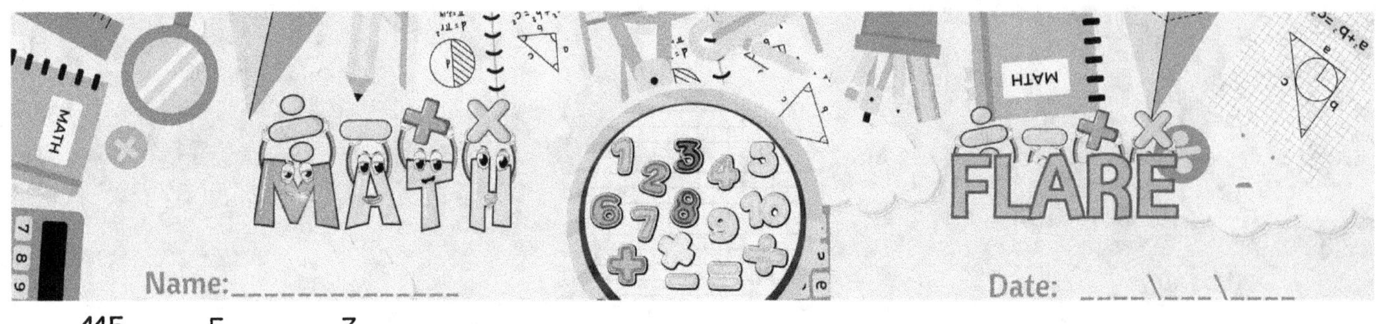

115. $6\frac{5}{10} + 6\frac{3}{6} =$ ________________________

116. $4\frac{2}{3} + 8\frac{6}{8} =$ ________________________

117. $8\frac{3}{4} - 5\frac{2}{5} =$ ________________________

118. $9\frac{1}{2} + 9\frac{6}{10} =$ ________________________

119. $4\frac{2}{9} + 6\frac{5}{7} =$ ________________________

120. $9\frac{3}{8} + 2\frac{2}{3} =$ ________________________

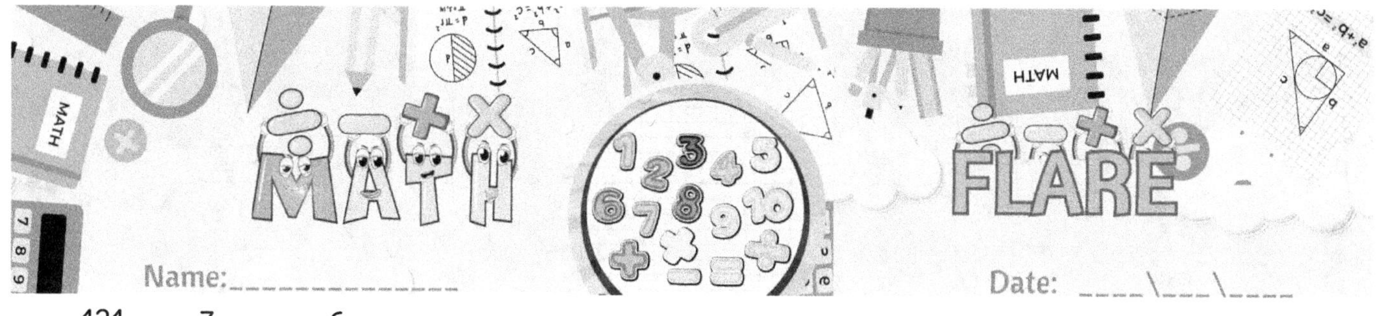

121. $9\frac{3}{4} - 4\frac{6}{9} =$ _______________________

122. $3\frac{8}{10} + 7\frac{1}{2} =$ _______________________

123. $7\frac{4}{5} + 7\frac{3}{6} =$ _______________________

124. $7\frac{4}{7} - 5\frac{1}{2} =$ _______________________

125. $5\frac{3}{9} - 2\frac{2}{3} =$ _______________________

126. $6\frac{1}{5} + 2\frac{5}{6} =$ _______________________

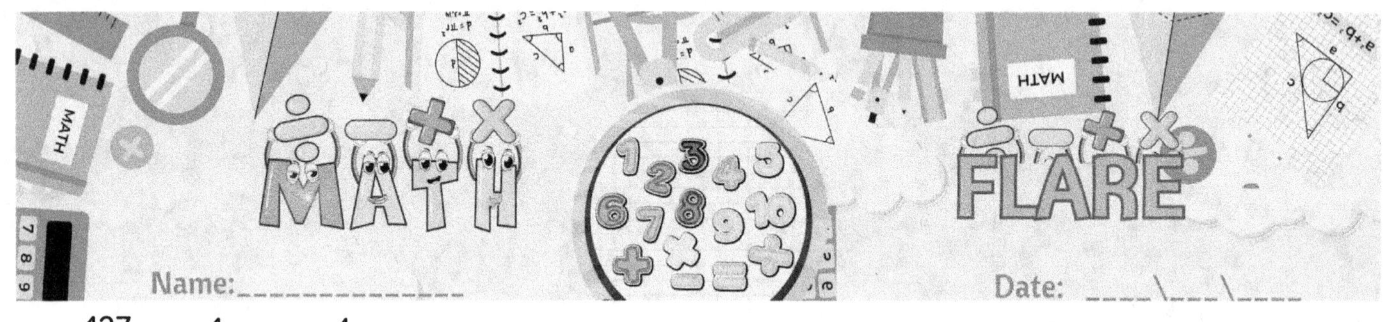

127. $8 \frac{4}{7} - 4 \frac{1}{4} =$ _______________

128. $9 \frac{7}{10} - 2 \frac{3}{8} =$ _______________

129. $8 \frac{4}{5} - 2 \frac{9}{10} =$ _______________

130. $3 \frac{3}{6} - 2 \frac{6}{8} =$ _______________

131. $8 \frac{2}{9} - 7 \frac{2}{3} =$ _______________

132. $9 \frac{1}{2} - 8 \frac{1}{7} =$ _______________

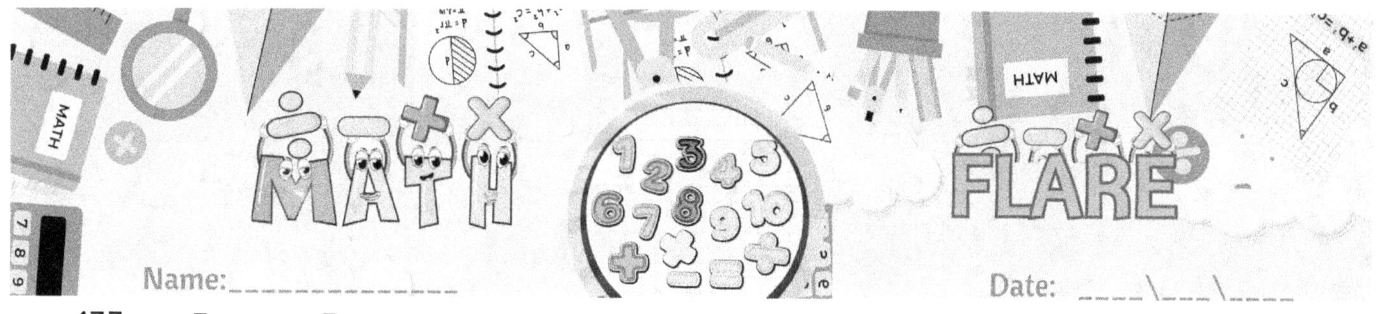

133. $7\frac{3}{4} - 5\frac{5}{8} =$ _______________

134. $1\frac{3}{4} + 3\frac{5}{6} =$ _______________

135. $6\frac{1}{3} - 2\frac{5}{10} =$ _______________

136. $9\frac{1}{2} - 6\frac{3}{5} =$ _______________

137. $3\frac{4}{7} + 8\frac{5}{9} =$ _______________

138. $8\frac{7}{8} - 8\frac{7}{9} =$ _______________

15

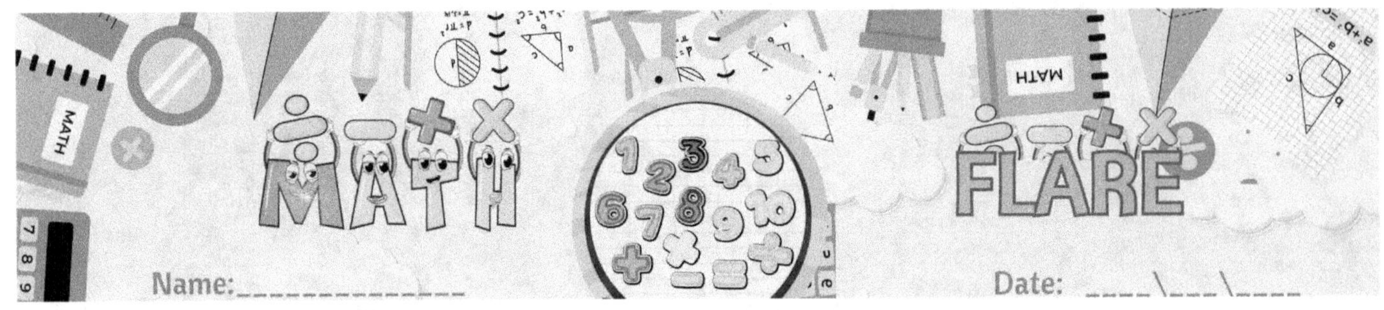

Mixed Numbers: Multiplication and Division

Calculate.

139. $8 \frac{5}{6} \div 6 \frac{2}{3} =$ _______________________________

140. $5 \frac{7}{10} \times 7 \frac{1}{2} =$ _______________________________

141. $2 \frac{2}{8} \times 4 \frac{2}{4} =$ _______________________________

142. $5 \frac{3}{5} \div 7 \frac{1}{3} =$ _______________________________

143. $3 \frac{4}{7} \div 9 \frac{2}{5} =$ _______________________________

144. $3 \frac{6}{8} \times 1 \frac{2}{10} =$ _______________________________

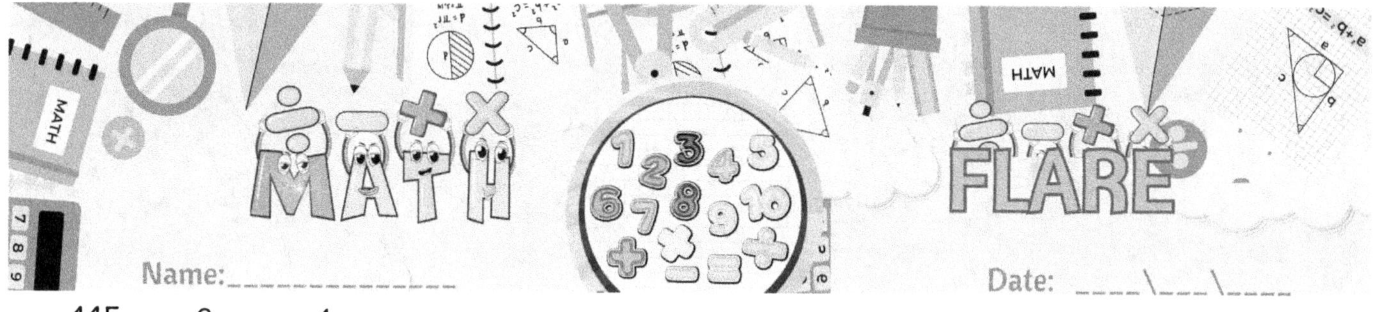

145. $4\frac{2}{6} \times 7\frac{1}{2} =$

146. $6\frac{4}{9} \div 2\frac{1}{4} =$

147. $9\frac{3}{9} \div 9\frac{5}{8} =$

148. $7\frac{3}{5} \times 9\frac{9}{10} =$

149. $3\frac{2}{3} \div 4\frac{2}{4} =$

150. $8\frac{4}{6} \div 9\frac{1}{2} =$

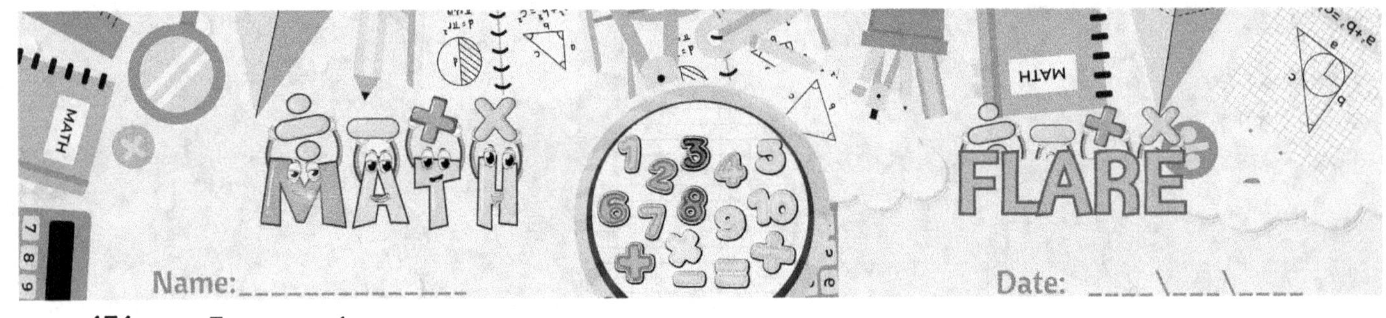

151. $9 \frac{5}{7} \div 3 \frac{1}{6} =$ _______________________

152. $6 \frac{3}{7} \times 5 \frac{4}{5} =$ _______________________

153. $8 \frac{2}{4} \div 8 \frac{8}{10} =$ _______________________

154. $5 \frac{5}{9} \times 5 \frac{1}{8} =$ _______________________

155. $9 \frac{2}{3} \times 9 \frac{1}{2} =$ _______________________

156. $4 \frac{1}{2} \div 9 \frac{2}{6} =$ _______________________

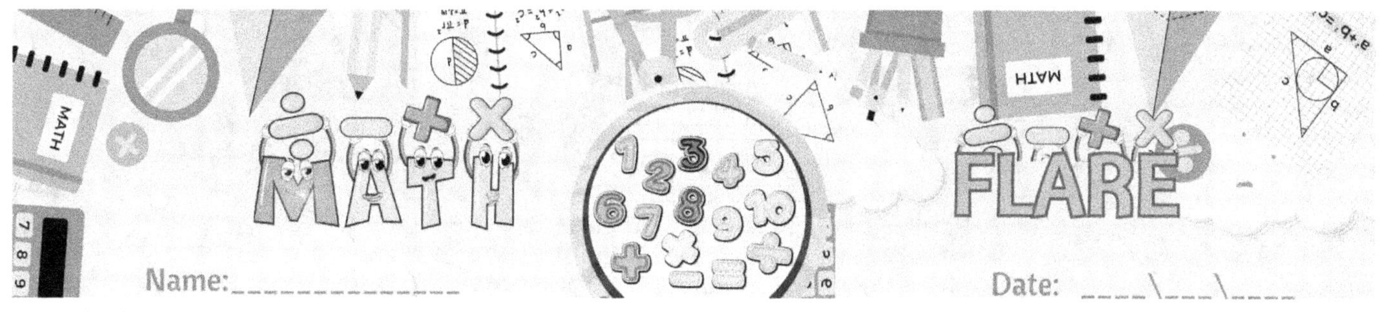

Name:_______________   Date: ____________

157. $3\frac{1}{7} \times 7\frac{2}{3} =$ ___________

158. $5\frac{3}{8} \times 4\frac{4}{10} =$ ___________

159. $9\frac{1}{4} \div 1\frac{2}{5} =$ ___________

160. $4\frac{6}{9} \times 3\frac{4}{8} =$ ___________

161. $5\frac{7}{9} \div 5\frac{2}{3} =$ ___________

162. $4\frac{3}{6} \div 8\frac{4}{5} =$ ___________

MathFlare - Fractions 5th and 6th Grade

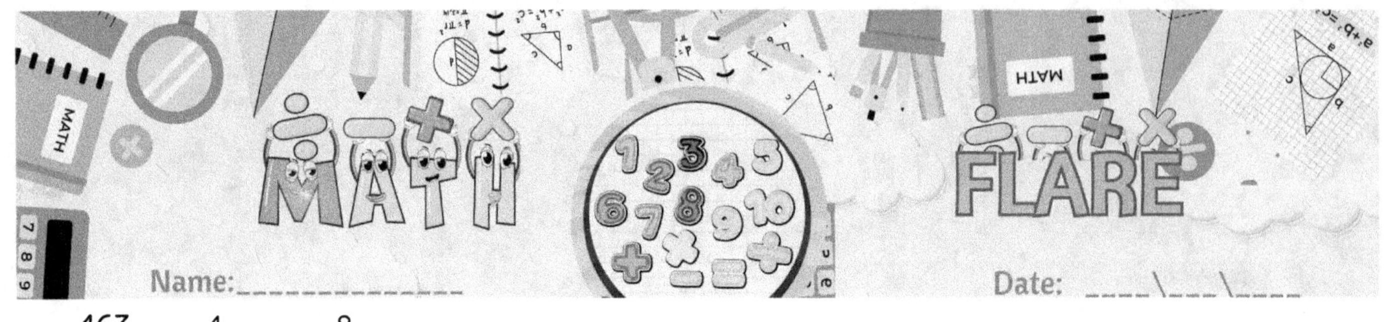

163. $8 \frac{1}{2} \times 5 \frac{8}{10} =$ _______________________

164. $3 \frac{5}{7} \times 2 \frac{3}{4} =$ _______________________

165. $7 \frac{1}{2} \times 4 \frac{8}{10} =$ _______________________

166. $4 \frac{1}{4} \times 5 \frac{2}{5} =$ _______________________

167. $4 \frac{7}{8} \div 2 \frac{3}{6} =$ _______________________

168. $2 \frac{4}{7} \times 2 \frac{2}{3} =$ _______________________

169. $3\frac{2}{9} \times 2\frac{3}{4} =$ _______________

170. $2\frac{8}{9} \div 6\frac{3}{8} =$ _______________

171. $3\frac{1}{5} \div 3\frac{6}{7} =$ _______________

172. $8\frac{1}{2} \times 5\frac{5}{6} =$ _______________

173. $4\frac{2}{3} \div 3\frac{1}{10} =$ _______________

174. $3\frac{1}{7} \div 8\frac{8}{9} =$ _______________

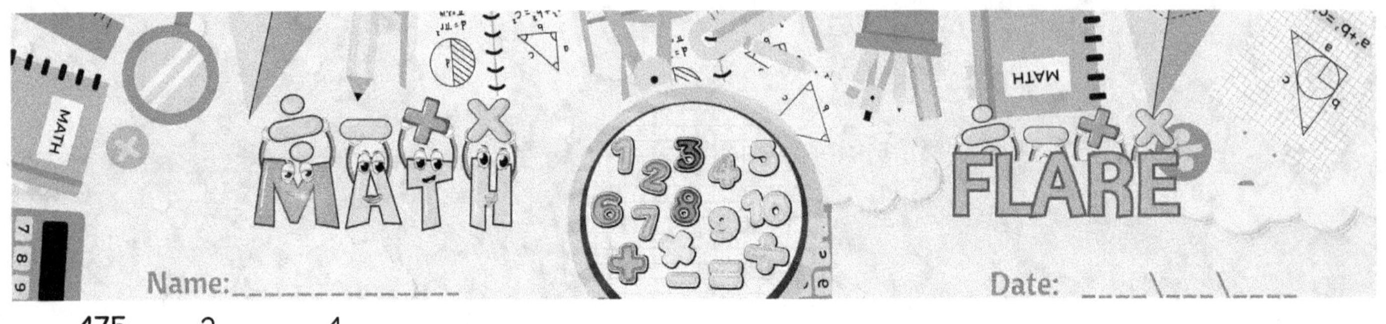

175. $2\frac{2}{4} \div 4\frac{1}{6} =$ _______________

176. $9\frac{6}{10} \div 9\frac{1}{2} =$ _______________

177. $9\frac{2}{3} \times 8\frac{2}{8} =$ _______________

178. $9\frac{4}{5} \times 7\frac{1}{4} =$ _______________

179. $5\frac{1}{2} \times 6\frac{1}{3} =$ _______________

180. $4\frac{4}{7} \times 4\frac{7}{8} =$ _______________

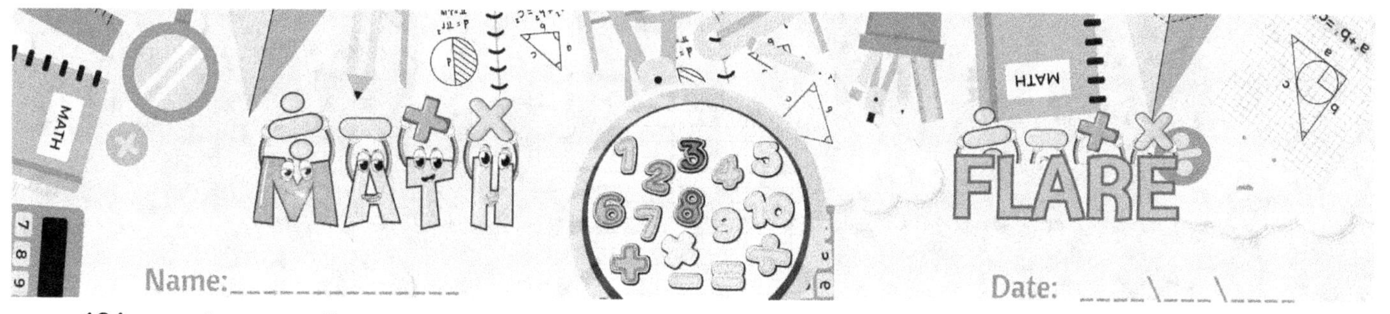

181. $1\frac{1}{10} \div 1\frac{5}{6} =$ _______________

182. $6\frac{3}{9} \times 6\frac{3}{5} =$ _______________

183. $2\frac{7}{9} \div 3\frac{6}{8} =$ _______________

184. $2\frac{2}{6} \times 7\frac{3}{10} =$ _______________

185. $6\frac{3}{4} \times 5\frac{1}{2} =$ _______________

186. $9\frac{6}{7} \div 9\frac{3}{5} =$ _______________

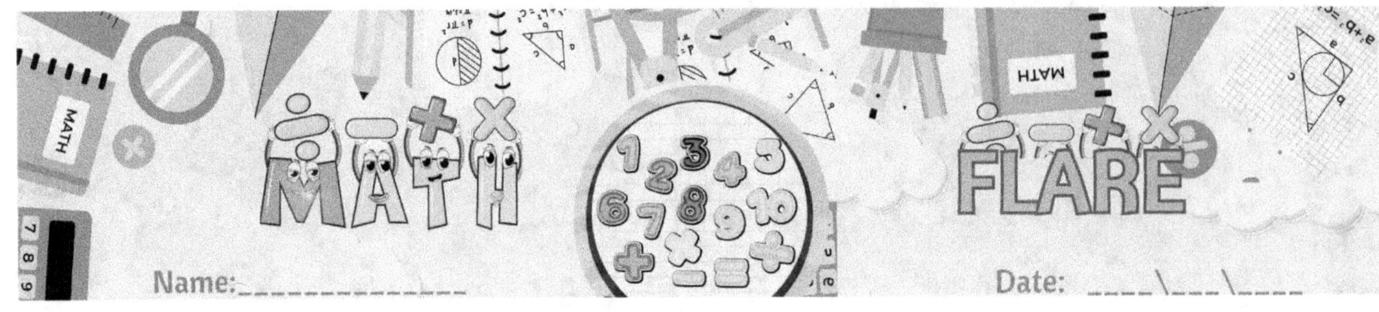

Multiplication with Whole Numbers

187. $\frac{6}{18}$ of 5 = _______________

188. $\frac{3}{6}$ of 7 = _______________

189. $\frac{4}{7}$ of 7 = _______________

190. $\frac{1}{4}$ of 3 = _______________

191. $5 \times \frac{9}{20}$ = _______________

192. $\frac{1}{8}$ of 6 = _______________

193. $1 \times \frac{1}{3}$ = _______________

194. $\frac{12}{13}$ of 4 = _______________

195. $\frac{3}{5}$ of 6 = _______________

196. $6 \times \frac{18}{19}$ = _______________

197. $\frac{9}{18}$ of 7 = _______________

198. $\frac{4}{6}$ of 9 = _______________

199. $\frac{1}{14}$ of 7 = _______________

200. $\frac{14}{17}$ of 2 = _______________

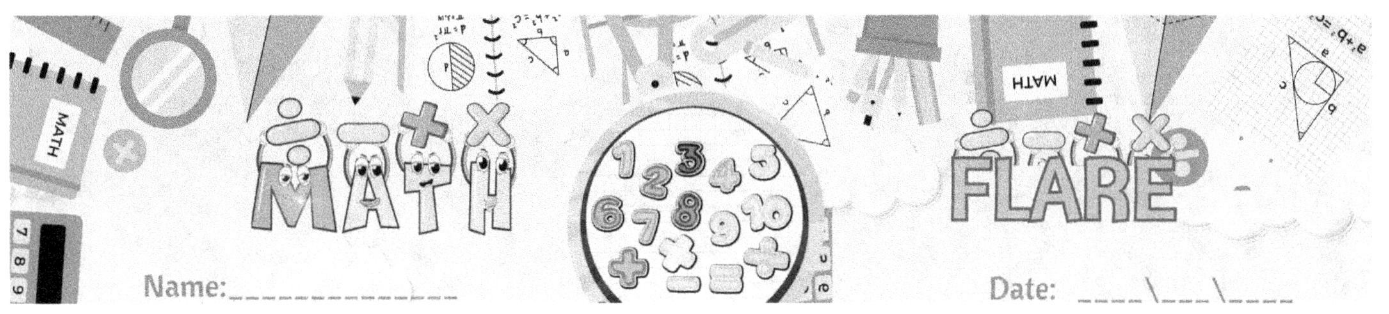

201. $4 \times \frac{8}{12} =$ ___________

202. $\frac{2}{8}$ of 4 = ___________

203. $\frac{2}{14}$ of 9 = ___________

204. $5 \times \frac{3}{4} =$ ___________

205. $\frac{6}{7}$ of 3 = ___________

206. $\frac{1}{11}$ of 7 = ___________

207. $\frac{9}{15}$ of 5 = ___________

208. $\frac{10}{17}$ of 5 = ___________

209. $7 \times \frac{4}{5} =$ ___________

210. $1 \times \frac{12}{13} =$ ___________

211. $3 \times \frac{10}{16} =$ ___________

212. $4 \times \frac{4}{10} =$ ___________

213. $5 \times \frac{6}{9} =$ ___________

214. $\frac{6}{18}$ of 8 = ___________

215. $5 \times \frac{14}{19} =$ ___________

216. $\frac{1}{20}$ of 8 = ___________

217. $1 \times \dfrac{1}{2} =$ ___________

218. $2 \times \dfrac{1}{3} =$ ___________

219. $1 \times \dfrac{4}{6} =$ ___________

220. $3 \times \dfrac{7}{9} =$ ___________

221. $2 \times \dfrac{1}{2} =$ ___________

222. $3 \times \dfrac{4}{6} =$ ___________

223. $\dfrac{2}{10}$ of $5 =$ ___________

224. $3 \times \dfrac{1}{16} =$ ___________

225. $\dfrac{16}{17}$ of $3 =$ ___________

226. $8 \times \dfrac{8}{19} =$ ___________

227. $\dfrac{3}{8}$ of $8 =$ ___________

228. $5 \times \dfrac{1}{14} =$ ___________

229. $6 \times \dfrac{18}{20} =$ ___________

230. $\dfrac{4}{12}$ of $6 =$ ___________

231. $\dfrac{1}{13}$ of $8 =$ ___________

232. $\dfrac{2}{3}$ of $6 =$ ___________

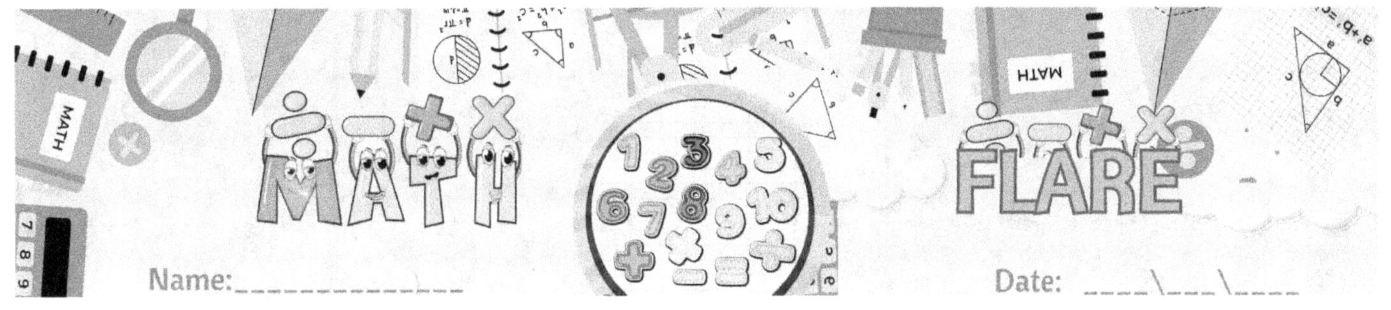

Simplify Fractions: Proper and Improper Fractions

233. $\dfrac{18}{36}$ = ___________________

234. $\dfrac{180}{36}$ = ___________________

235. $\dfrac{12}{18}$ = ___________________

236. $\dfrac{38}{4}$ = ___________________

237. $\dfrac{680}{85}$ = ___________________

238. $\dfrac{105}{12}$ = ___________________

239. $\dfrac{160}{80}$ = ___________________

240. $\dfrac{6}{24}$ = ___________________

241. $\dfrac{330}{55}$ = ___________________

242. $\dfrac{112}{56}$ = ___________________

243. $\dfrac{40}{72}$ = ___________________

244. $\dfrac{205}{25}$ = ___________________

245. $\dfrac{2}{26}$ = _______________

246. $\dfrac{10}{40}$ = _______________

247. $\dfrac{396}{135}$ = _______________

248. $\dfrac{1197}{133}$ = _______________

249. $\dfrac{49}{70}$ = _______________

250. $\dfrac{24}{72}$ = _______________

251. $\dfrac{128}{16}$ = _______________

252. $\dfrac{44}{6}$ = _______________

253. $\dfrac{392}{56}$ = _______________

254. $\dfrac{945}{135}$ = _______________

255. $\dfrac{276}{40}$ = _______________

256. $\dfrac{20}{10}$ = _______________

257. $\dfrac{630}{126}$ = _______________

258. $\dfrac{24}{36}$ = _______________

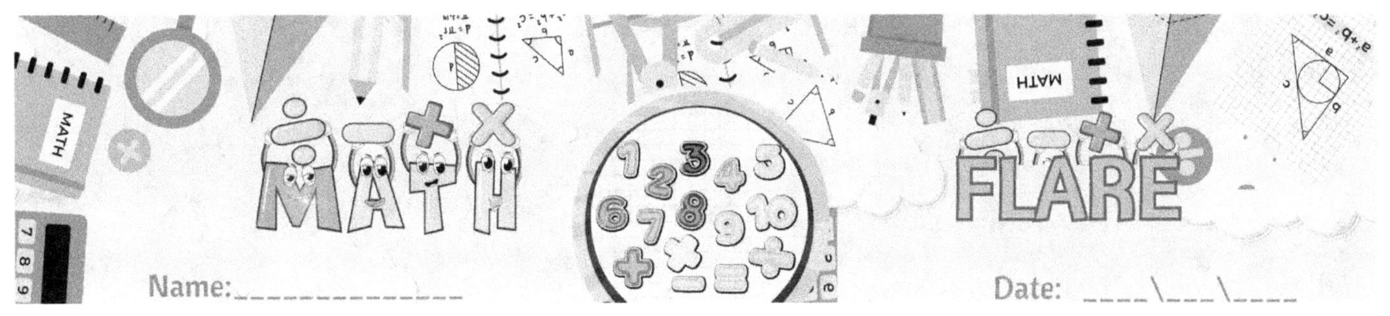

259. $\dfrac{520}{128}$ = _______________

260. $\dfrac{20}{44}$ = _______________

261. $\dfrac{198}{57}$ = _______________

262. $\dfrac{27}{36}$ = _______________

263. $\dfrac{196}{28}$ = _______________

264. $\dfrac{468}{52}$ = _______________

265. $\dfrac{3}{6}$ = _______________

266. $\dfrac{35}{85}$ = _______________

267. $\dfrac{192}{42}$ = _______________

268. $\dfrac{9}{90}$ = _______________

269. $\dfrac{917}{112}$ = _______________

270. $\dfrac{6}{9}$ = _______________

271. $\dfrac{180}{45}$ = _______________

272. $\dfrac{196}{49}$ = _______________

MathFlare - Fractions 5th and 6th Grade

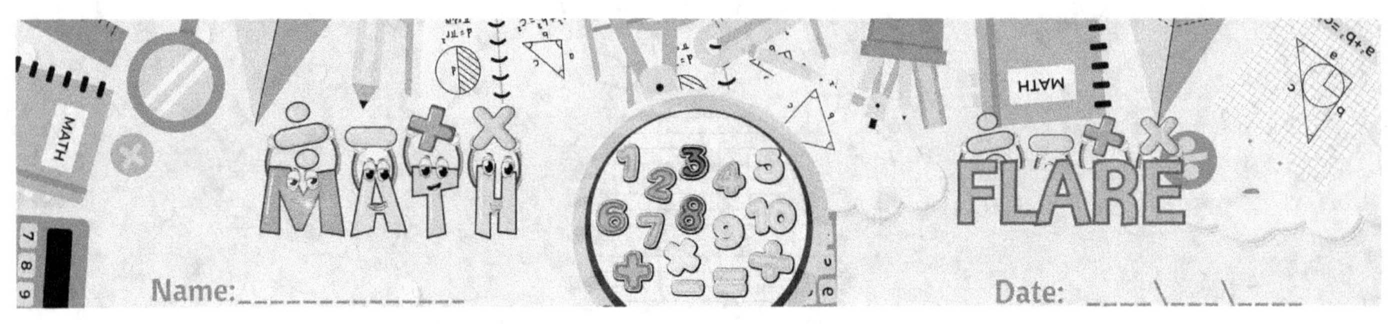

273. $\dfrac{12}{42}$ = _______________

274. $\dfrac{105}{30}$ = _______________

275. $\dfrac{48}{6}$ = _______________

276. $\dfrac{474}{54}$ = _______________

277. $\dfrac{182}{35}$ = _______________

278. $\dfrac{50}{55}$ = _______________

279. $\dfrac{1188}{171}$ = _______________

280. $\dfrac{180}{90}$ = _______________

281. $\dfrac{45}{65}$ = _______________

282. $\dfrac{312}{48}$ = _______________

283. $\dfrac{1377}{153}$ = _______________

284. $\dfrac{26}{8}$ = _______________

285. $\dfrac{378}{108}$ = _______________

286. $\dfrac{177}{60}$ = _______________

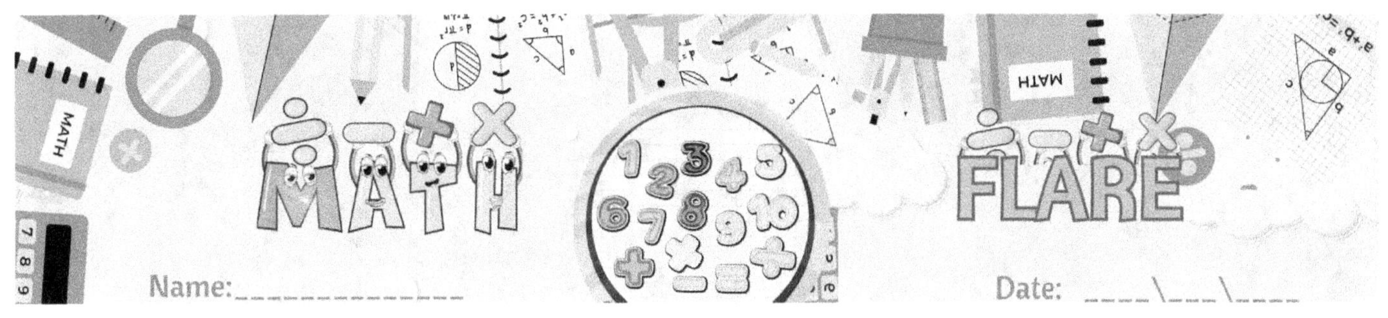

287. $\dfrac{468}{162} =$ _______________

288. $\dfrac{102}{42} =$ _______________

289. $\dfrac{438}{120} =$ _______________

290. $\dfrac{198}{27} =$ _______________

291. $\dfrac{434}{91} =$ _______________

292. $\dfrac{90}{18} =$ _______________

293. $\dfrac{108}{18} =$ _______________

294. $\dfrac{504}{56} =$ _______________

295. $\dfrac{298}{34} =$ _______________

296. $\dfrac{9}{12} =$ _______________

297. $\dfrac{224}{40} =$ _______________

298. $\dfrac{1192}{152} =$ _______________

299. $\dfrac{25}{55} =$ _______________

300. $\dfrac{24}{6} =$ _______________

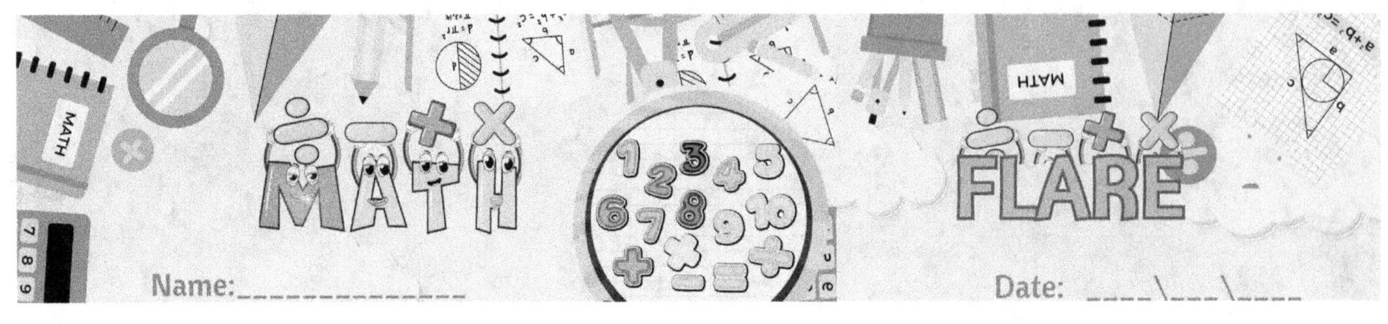

301. $\dfrac{24}{30} =$ _______________

302. $\dfrac{45}{126} =$ _______________

303. $\dfrac{4}{64} =$ _______________

304. $\dfrac{12}{40} =$ _______________

305. $\dfrac{672}{84} =$ _______________

306. $\dfrac{567}{153} =$ _______________

307. $\dfrac{84}{28} =$ _______________

308. $\dfrac{12}{48} =$ _______________

309. $\dfrac{480}{57} =$ _______________

310. $\dfrac{14}{49} =$ _______________

311. $\dfrac{720}{75} =$ _______________

312. $\dfrac{30}{32} =$ _______________

313. $\dfrac{360}{72} =$ _______________

314. $\dfrac{21}{77} =$ _______________

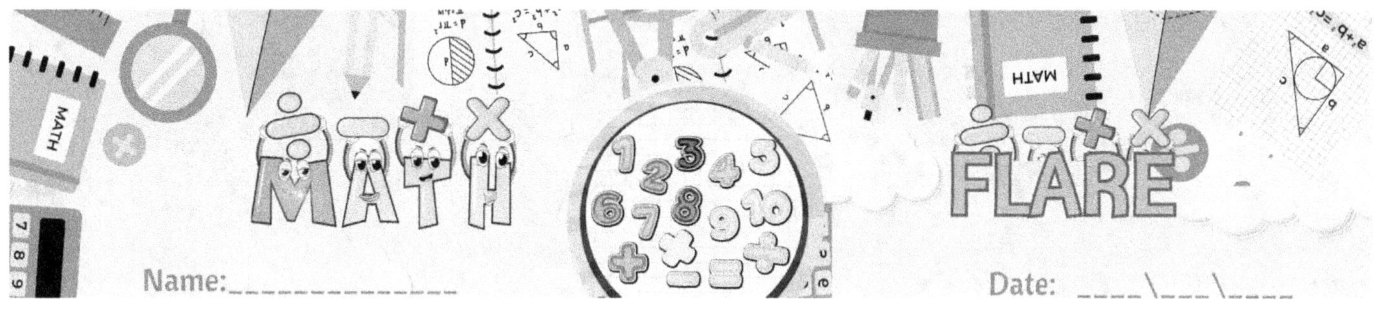

Name:_______________   Date: _______________

Multiple Operations Fractions

Find the solution.

315. $\dfrac{3}{5} + \dfrac{1}{6} + 5 =$

316. $\dfrac{5}{6} + \dfrac{3}{7} + 7 =$

317. $\dfrac{3}{10} + \dfrac{1}{7} - \dfrac{1}{4} =$

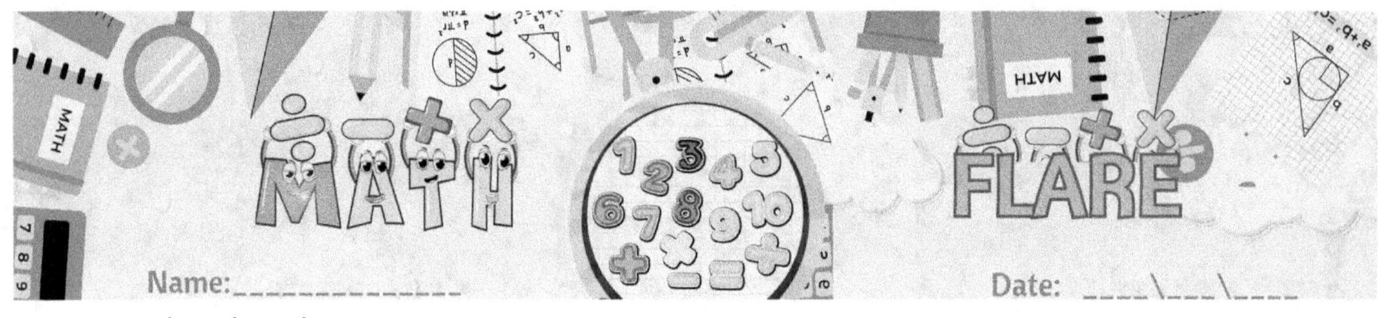

318. $\dfrac{1}{2} \times \dfrac{1}{3} + \dfrac{4}{7} =$

319. $\left(\dfrac{1}{5} + \dfrac{1}{4}\right) - \left(\dfrac{1}{7} \times \dfrac{6}{7}\right) =$

320. $\left(\dfrac{1}{2} + \dfrac{1}{2}\right) \times \left(\dfrac{3}{8} + \dfrac{3}{4}\right) =$

321. $\dfrac{2}{3} \times \dfrac{1}{3} \times \dfrac{2}{3} =$

322. $\dfrac{2}{9} + \dfrac{2}{5} + \dfrac{1}{2} =$

323. $\dfrac{5}{8} + \dfrac{5}{7} + \dfrac{5}{7} + \dfrac{3}{5} =$

324. $\dfrac{1}{2} \times \dfrac{3}{8} + \dfrac{1}{4} =$

325. $\dfrac{1}{7} + \dfrac{3}{4} + 8 =$

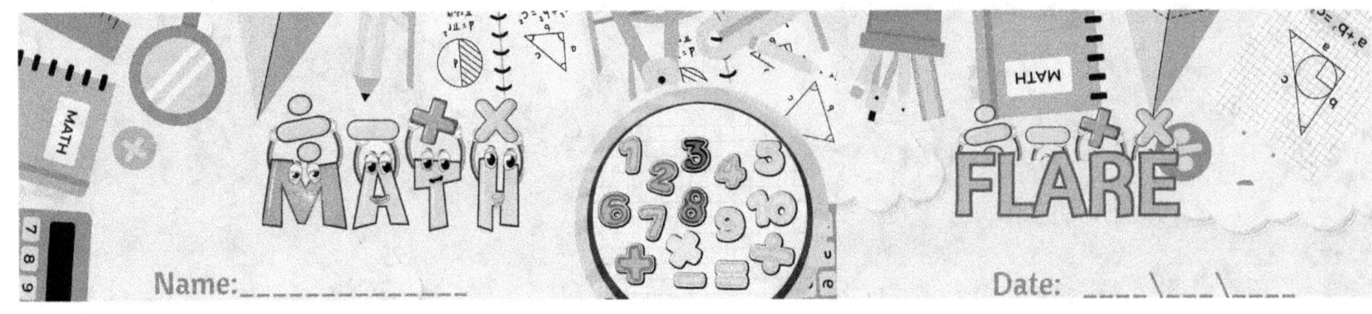

326. $\dfrac{2}{3} + \dfrac{1}{2} + 5 =$

327. $\dfrac{1}{3} \times \dfrac{1}{10} + \dfrac{1}{8} =$

328. $\left(\dfrac{1}{3} + \dfrac{5}{9} \right) - \left(\dfrac{2}{3} \times \dfrac{1}{4} \right) =$

329. $\left(\dfrac{7}{10} + \dfrac{1}{2} \right) \div \dfrac{6}{7} =$

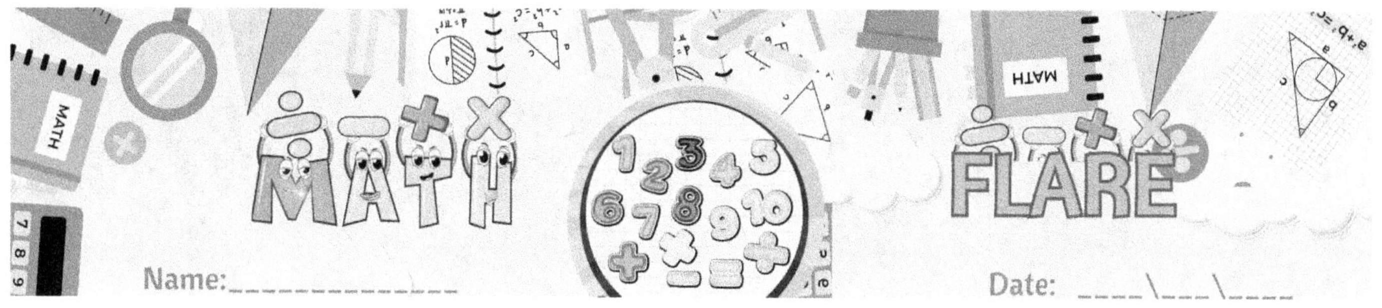

330. $\dfrac{5}{8} \times \dfrac{1}{3} + \dfrac{1}{4} =$

331. $\left(\dfrac{1}{2} \times \dfrac{2}{3}\right) + \left(\dfrac{1}{5} \times \dfrac{3}{10}\right) =$

332. $\left(\dfrac{1}{3} \times \dfrac{2}{7}\right) + \left(\dfrac{1}{2} \times \dfrac{1}{2}\right) =$

333. $\dfrac{8}{9} + \dfrac{4}{5} + \dfrac{1}{4} + \dfrac{2}{3} =$

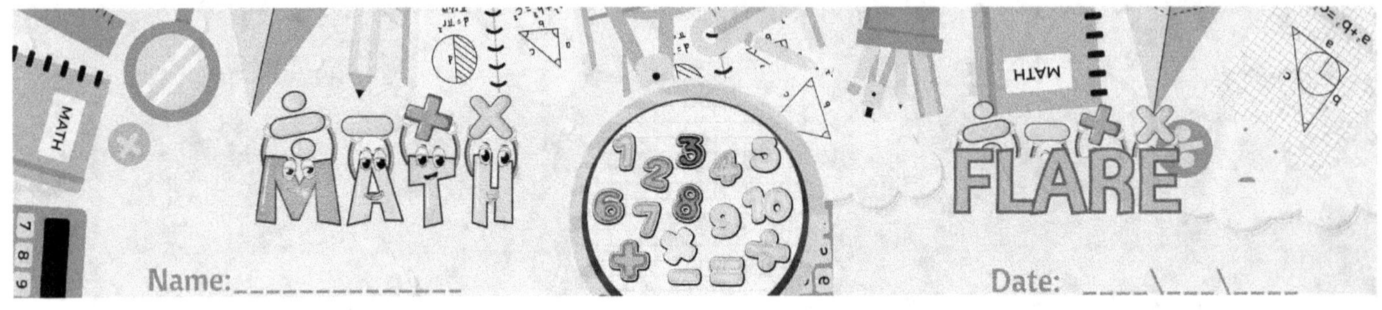

334. $\left(\dfrac{7}{9} + \dfrac{1}{6}\right) \times \left(\dfrac{2}{7} + \dfrac{1}{6}\right) =$

335. $\dfrac{1}{6} + \dfrac{2}{9} + \dfrac{1}{10} + \dfrac{1}{8} =$

336. $\dfrac{7}{9} + \dfrac{1}{3} + 6 =$

337. $\dfrac{2}{5} + \dfrac{8}{9} - \dfrac{4}{5} =$

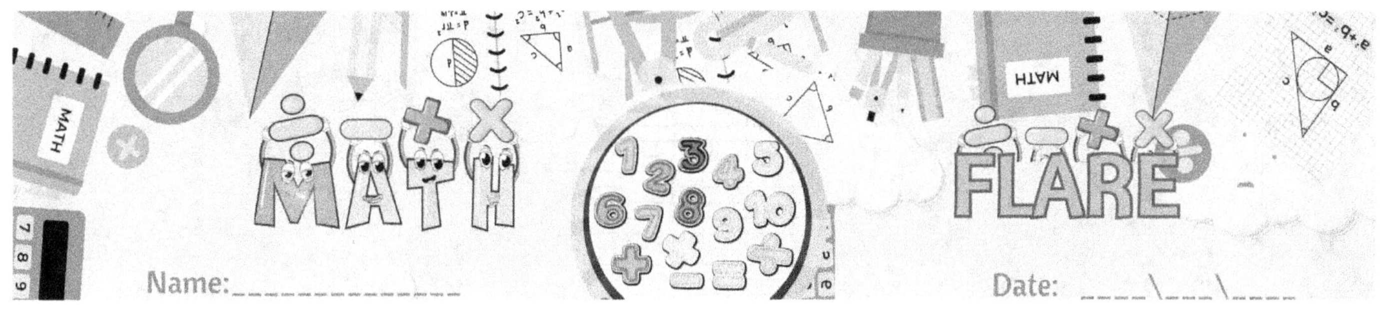

338. $\left(\frac{1}{4} \times \frac{1}{4}\right) + \left(\frac{5}{8} \times \frac{3}{5}\right) =$

339. $\frac{5}{8} + \frac{1}{7} + 4 =$

340. $\frac{2}{5} + \frac{1}{2} + \frac{1}{4} + \frac{1}{5} =$

341. $\frac{7}{10} + \frac{2}{3} + 6 =$

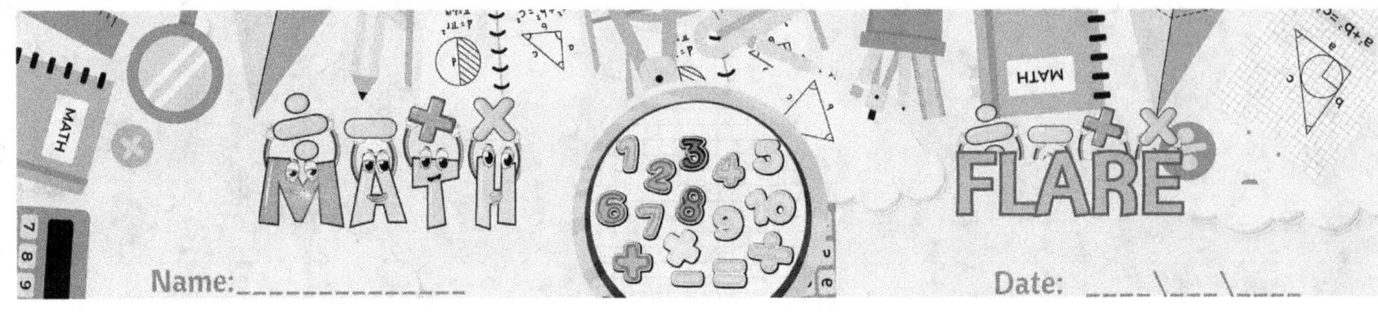

342. $\dfrac{2}{9} + \dfrac{5}{8} - \dfrac{2}{9} =$

343. $\dfrac{1}{4} \times \dfrac{8}{9} + \dfrac{5}{7} =$

344. $\left(\dfrac{5}{6} + \dfrac{5}{8} \right) \div \dfrac{5}{8} =$

345. $\dfrac{1}{6} + \dfrac{1}{5} + \dfrac{5}{9} =$

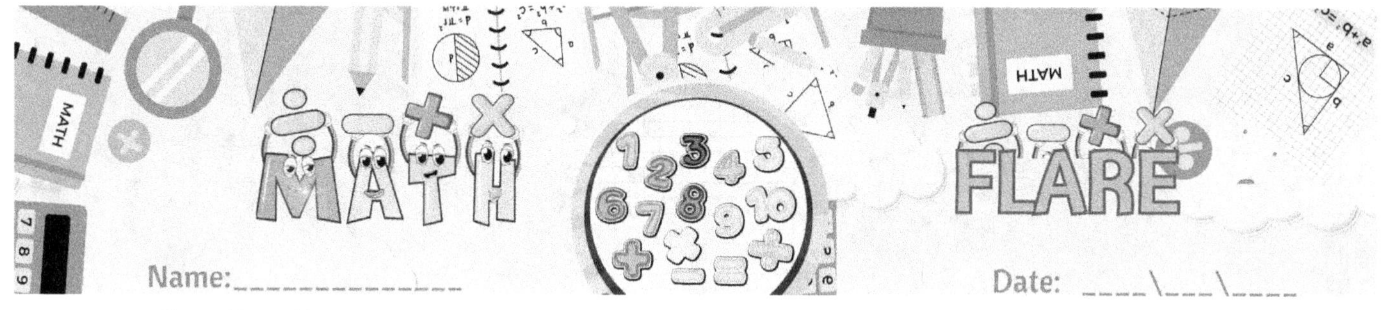

346. $\dfrac{3}{5} + \dfrac{5}{6} + \dfrac{5}{7} =$

347. $\left(\dfrac{1}{8} + \dfrac{1}{8} \right) \div \dfrac{3}{5} =$

348. $\left(\dfrac{2}{7} + \dfrac{1}{10} \right) \div \dfrac{3}{4} =$

349. $\dfrac{8}{9} + \dfrac{1}{9} - \dfrac{2}{9} =$

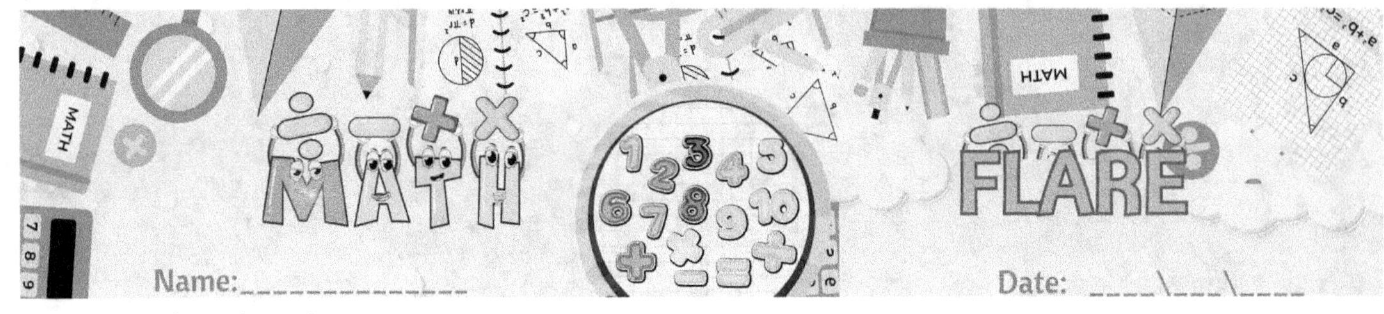

350. $\dfrac{2}{9} + \dfrac{1}{5} + \dfrac{1}{6} =$

351. $\dfrac{3}{5} + \dfrac{1}{2} + 9 =$

352. $\dfrac{1}{7} + \dfrac{1}{3} + 5 =$

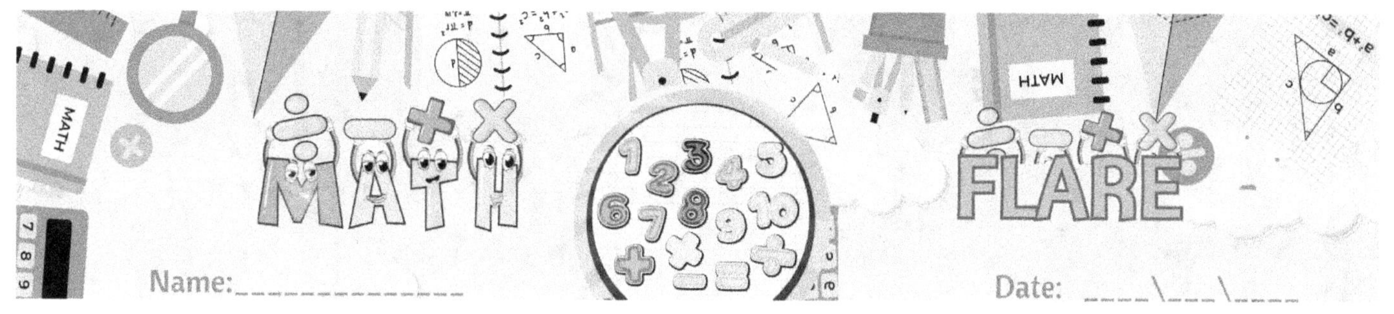

Fractions Addition Word Problems

353. Colton rode $\frac{2}{6}$ of a mile on his bike and then ran $\frac{5}{8}$ of a mile. How far did he travel in total?

354. Brandon drank $\frac{1}{2}$ of a bottle of juice and then drank another $\frac{2}{5}$ of the bottle later. How much of the bottle did he drink in total?

355. Addison cycled $\frac{1}{4}$ miles. She then stopped to buy some groceries. Then she cycled $\frac{3}{6}$ more miles. How far did Addison cycle in total?

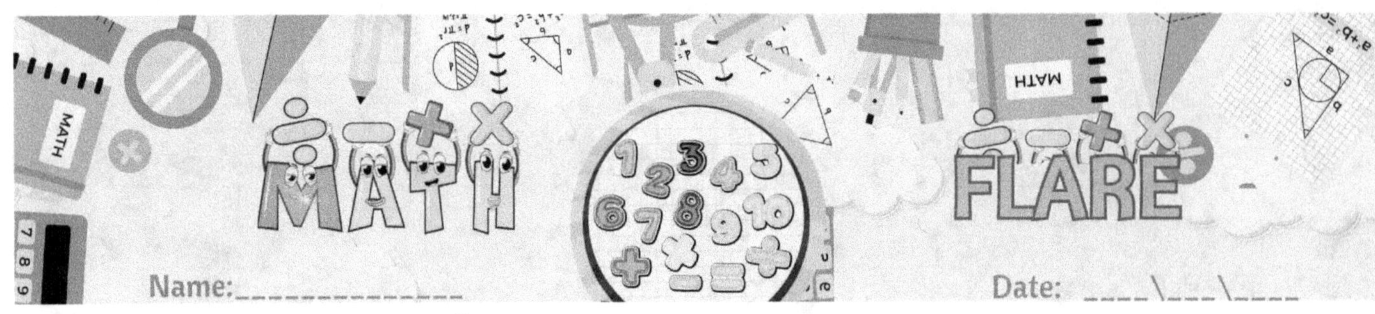

356. Natalie extracts $\frac{2}{6}$ of a glass of orange juice and then added $\frac{2}{4}$ of a glass of apple juice. How much juice is in the glass in total?

357. Wesley ran $\frac{2}{7}$ of a mile and then walked another $\frac{3}{9}$ of a mile. How far did he travel in total?

358. What is $\frac{2}{9}$ plus $\frac{2}{8}$?

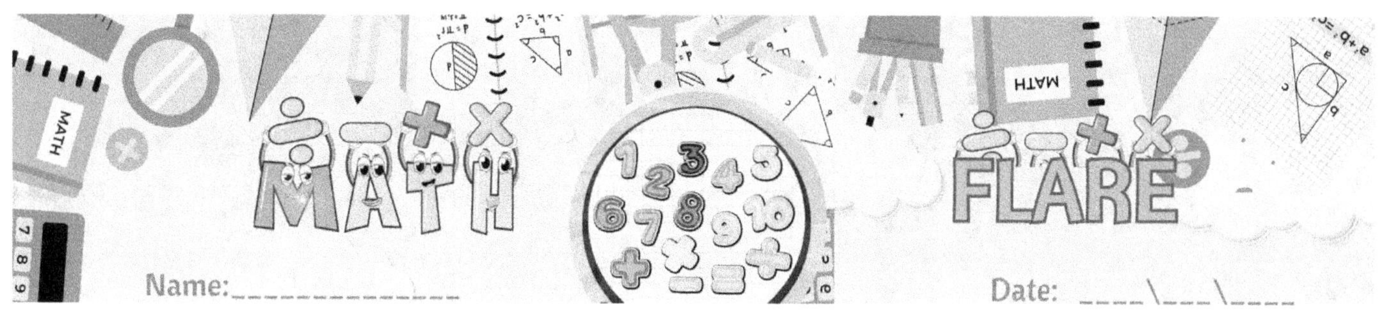

Name:______________________   Date: _______________

359. Chloe used $\frac{1}{6}$ of a stick of butter in a recipe and then used another $\frac{1}{3}$ of the stick in a different recipe. How much of the stick did she use in total?

360. Paisley knitted $\frac{1}{2}$ of a scarf and then $\frac{1}{4}$ of the same scarf. How much of the scarf has she knitted so far?

361. What is the sum of $\frac{2}{7}$ and $\frac{2}{7}$?

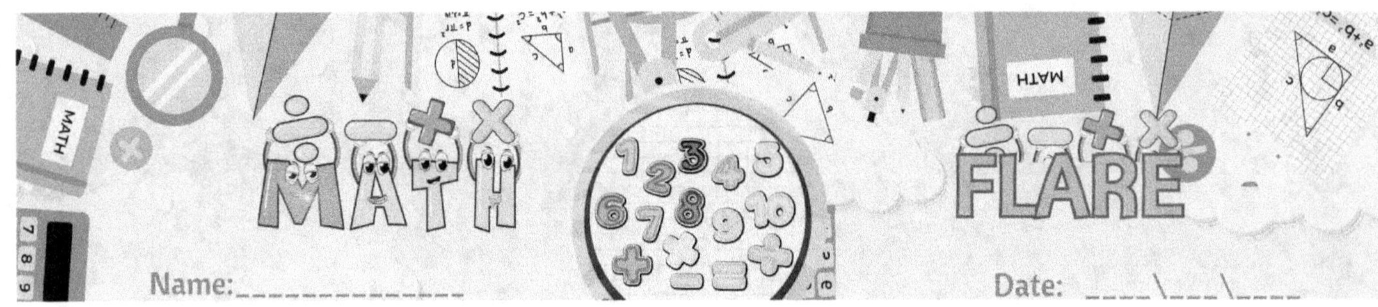

362. A snack mix recipe calls for $\frac{4}{5}$ cups of almonds and $\frac{1}{8}$ cups of peanuts. How much snack mix is needed in total?

363. A recipe calls for $\frac{2}{8}$ cups of milk and $\frac{2}{4}$ cups of cream. How much liquid in total is needed for the recipe?

364. Noah jogged $\frac{1}{2}$ of a mile in the morning and then jogged another $\frac{1}{7}$ of a mile in the evening. How much did he jog in total?

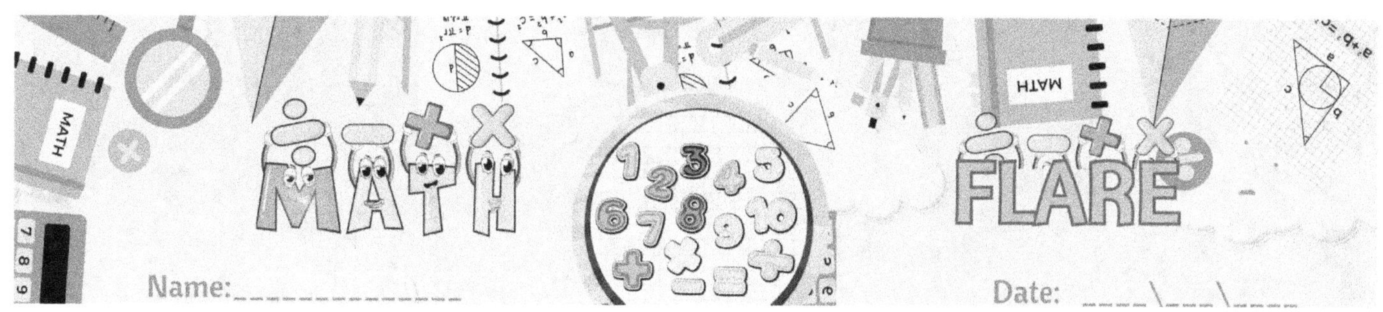

365. Carter writes $\frac{3}{10}$ of his paper before lunch. After lunch, he writes $\frac{1}{3}$ more. How much of his paper has he finished in total?

366. Lincoln solved $\frac{2}{9}$ of a math quiz and then $\frac{4}{6}$ of the same quiz. How much of the quiz has she solved?

367. Naomi baked $\frac{1}{5}$ of a cakes for her friend's birthday. She then baked $\frac{2}{10}$ of cookies. How much did she bake in total?

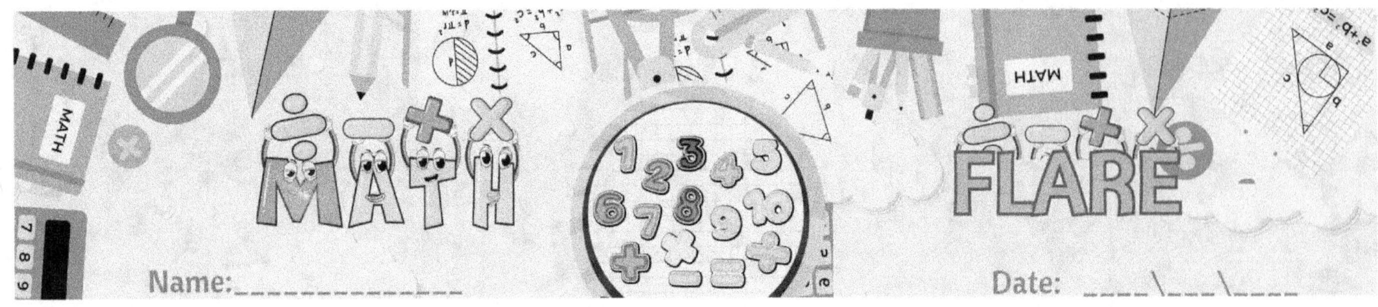

368. Brody paints $\frac{2}{6}$ of his paintnig on Monday, and $\frac{1}{4}$ on Tuesday. How much of his painting has he finished in total?

369. A recipe calls for $\frac{5}{10}$ cups of peanut butter and $\frac{1}{5}$ cups of jelly. How much of the ingredients are needed in total for the recipe?

370. Isabella read $\frac{2}{4}$ pages of her book before bed. She then read another $\frac{2}{6}$ pages before falling asleep. How much of her book did she read in total?

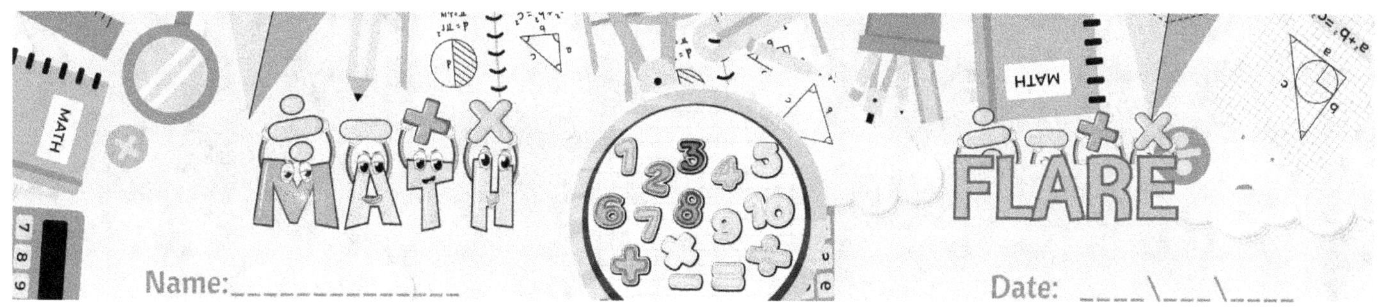

371. Emily made a salad with $\frac{2}{8}$ of a cup of lettuce and $\frac{6}{10}$ of a cup of spinach. How much salad did she make in total?

372. Genesis drove $\frac{2}{8}$ miles. She then stopped to have some coffee. Then she drove $\frac{5}{9}$ more miles. How far did Genesis drive in total?

373. Easton drank $\frac{1}{2}$ of a bottle of water and then drank another $\frac{1}{2}$ of the bottle later. How much of the bottle did he drink in total?

Fractions Subtraction Word Problems

374. Ayden has a board that is $\frac{2}{8}$ feet long. He wants to cut off $\frac{2}{10}$ of the board. How long will the board be after the cut?

375. A recipe calls for $\frac{6}{10}$ of a cup of sugar. If $\frac{4}{9}$ of the sugar is already used, how much sugar is left in cups?

376. Nolan has a length of ribbon that is $\frac{3}{5}$ meters long. He wants to cut off $\frac{1}{8}$ of the ribbon to use for a gift. How long will the remaining ribbon be?

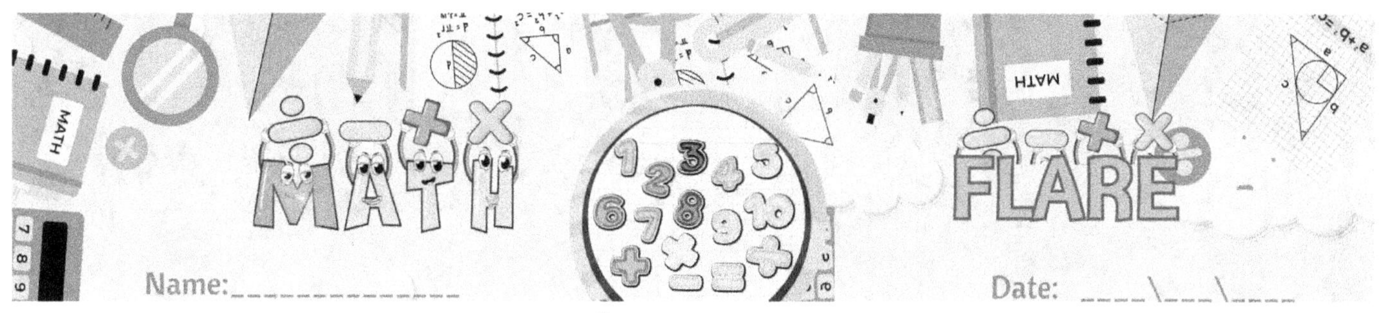

377. Olivia has a book that is $\frac{2}{3}$ of an inch thick. She reads $\frac{1}{3}$ of the book. How thick is the remaining portion of the book in inches?

378. Scarlett needs $\frac{7}{9}$ of a pound of cheese to make pizza. She only has $\frac{5}{9}$ of a pound of cheese. How much more cheese does she need to buy?

379. A recipe calls for $\frac{8}{10}$ of a cup of milk. If $\frac{1}{9}$ of the milk is already used, how much milk is left in cups?

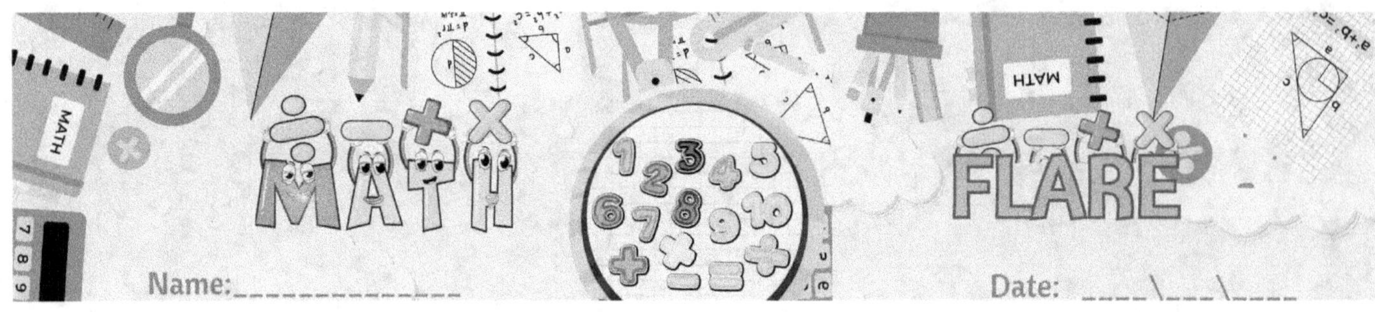

380. Ariana is painting a room with a can of paint that has $\frac{4}{5}$ gallons in it. She has used $\frac{2}{4}$ of the paint so far. How much paint is left in the can?

381. Isabella has $\frac{3}{4}$ of a pound of flour. She uses $\frac{6}{10}$ of the flour to make a pencake. How much flour is left in pounds?

382. Jordan has a rope that is $\frac{2}{5}$ of a foot long. He cuts $\frac{1}{3}$ of the rope. How long is the remaining rope in feet?

383. Brielle bought $\frac{1}{2}$ of a pound of peanuts. After sharing $\frac{1}{4}$ of the peanuts with her friend, how many pounds of peanuts did Brielle have left?

384. Jace has $\frac{7}{8}$ of a pound of cheese. He uses $\frac{6}{8}$ of the cheese to make a sandwich. How much cheese is left in pounds?

385. Lincoln has a collection of needles that weighs $\frac{5}{6}$ of a pound. If he loses $\frac{6}{9}$ of the weight, how much does the collection now weigh in pounds?

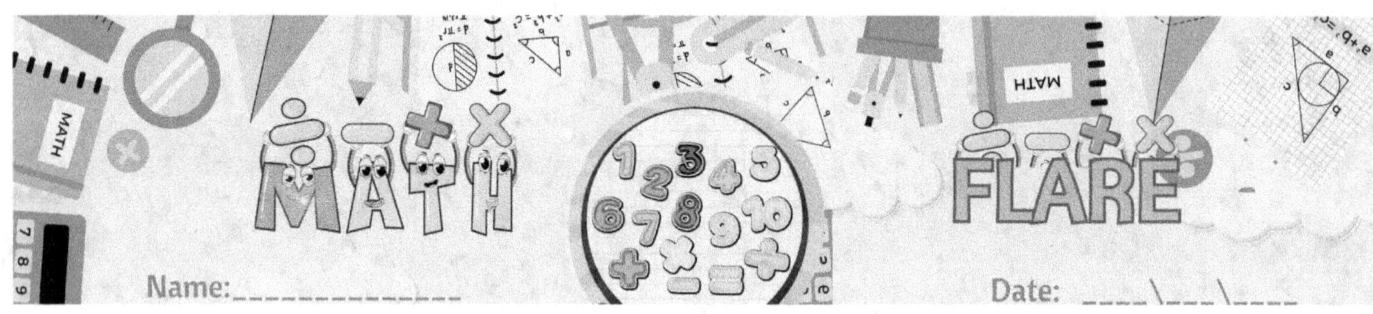

386. Xavier has a rope that is $\frac{1}{2}$ of a meter long. He needs to cut off $\frac{1}{4}$ of a meter to tie a knot. How long is the rope after the knot is tied?

387. Alexa had a cake that weighed $\frac{1}{3}$ of a pound. She cut off $\frac{1}{8}$ of a pound to share with her friends. How much cake does she have left?

388. A container has $\frac{2}{7}$ of a gallon of milk. If $\frac{1}{6}$ of the milk is taken out and put into another container, how much milk is left in the original container in gallons?

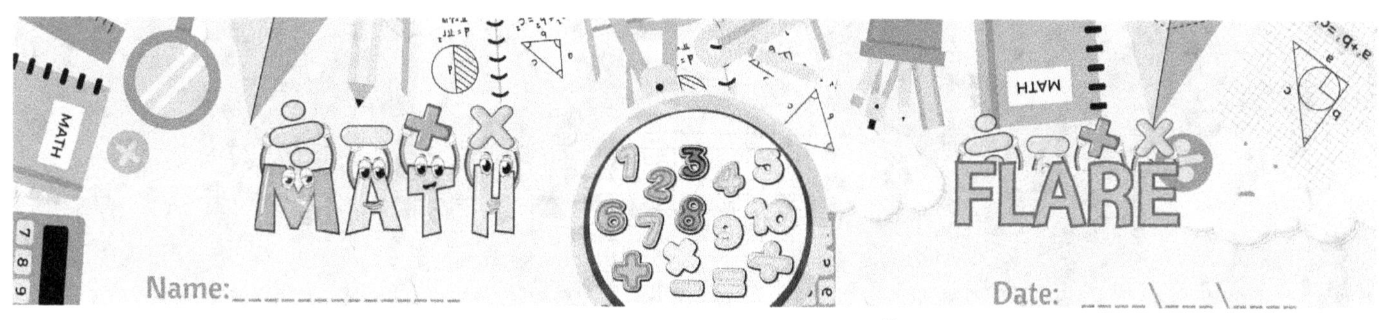

389. Piper is making a sweet dish and needs $\frac{9}{10}$ of a cup of strawberries. She has already used $\frac{8}{10}$ of a cup. How much more strawberry does she need?

390. Tristan has $\frac{2}{3}$ of a bag of rulers. He takes out $\frac{5}{9}$ of the rulers. How many rulers are in the bag now?

391. Nathaniel has $\frac{1}{2}$ of a pizza left over from last night. He eats $\frac{4}{10}$ of the pizza for lunch. How much pizza does he have left?

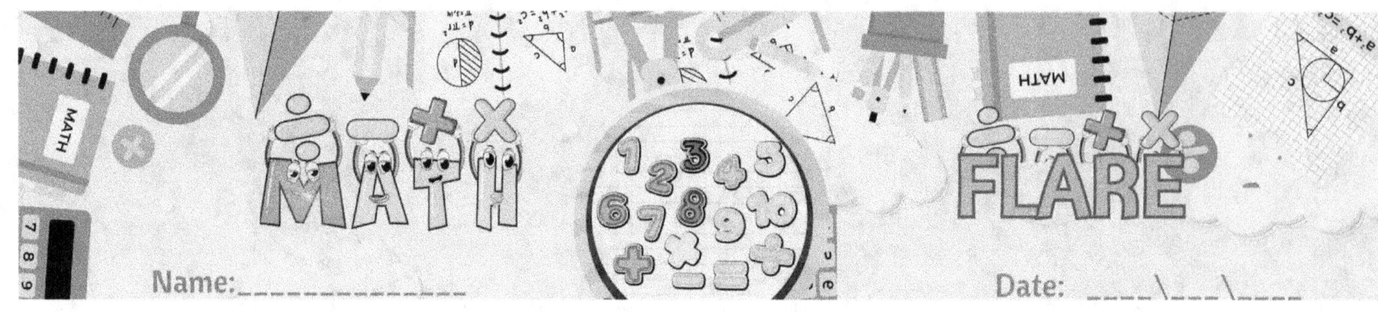

392. Emma is running on a track that is $\frac{4}{9}$ of a mile long. She has already run $\frac{1}{4}$ of the mile. How much further does she have to run?

393. Landon and Eva are cooking dinner and need $\frac{3}{6}$ of a cup of oil. Landon accidentally spills $\frac{4}{10}$ of a cup of oil. How much oil do they have left?

394. Madison had $\frac{1}{5}$ of a cup of milk. If $\frac{1}{8}$ of the milk is spilled, how much milk is left in cups?

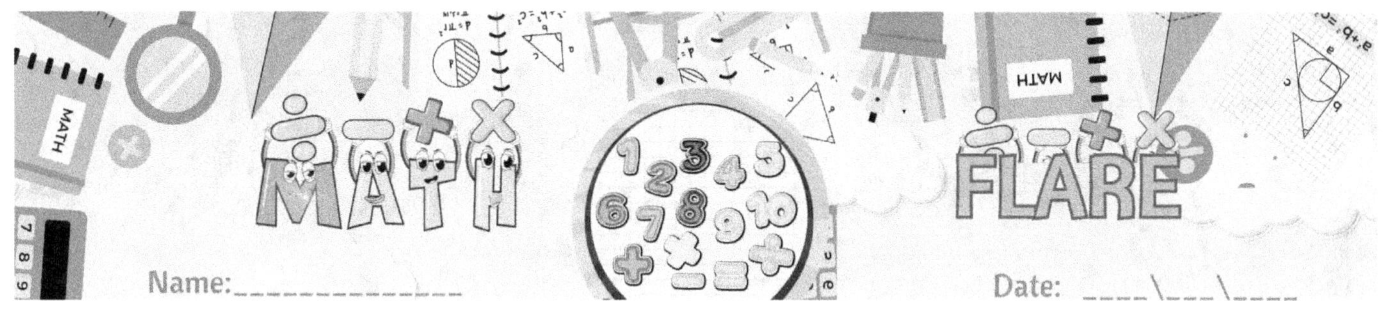

Fractions Multiplication Word Problems

395. If a cake recipe calls for $\frac{2}{7}$ cup of flour and you want to make 4 cakes, how much flour do you need?

396. Nicholas is making a dish that calls for $\frac{3}{6}$ cup of cooking oil. If he wants to make 2 dishes of the same recipe, how much cooking oil does he need?

397. If you need to make 5 batches of cookies, and each batch requires $\frac{4}{8}$ cup of chocolate chips, how many cups of chocolate chips do you need in total?

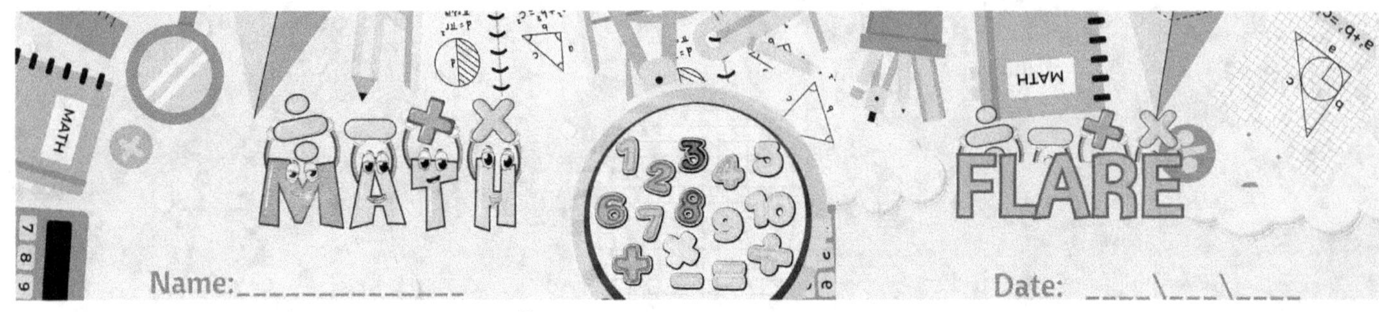

398. If a recipe calls for $\frac{7}{10}$ cup of sugar to make 1 dozen cookies, how much sugar is needed to make 4 dozen cookies?

399. If a recipe calls for $\frac{2}{3}$ cup of milk and you want to make $\frac{5}{10}$ times as much, how much milk do you need?

400. A basketball team wins $\frac{6}{9}$ of their games. If they play 10 games in a season, how many games did they win?

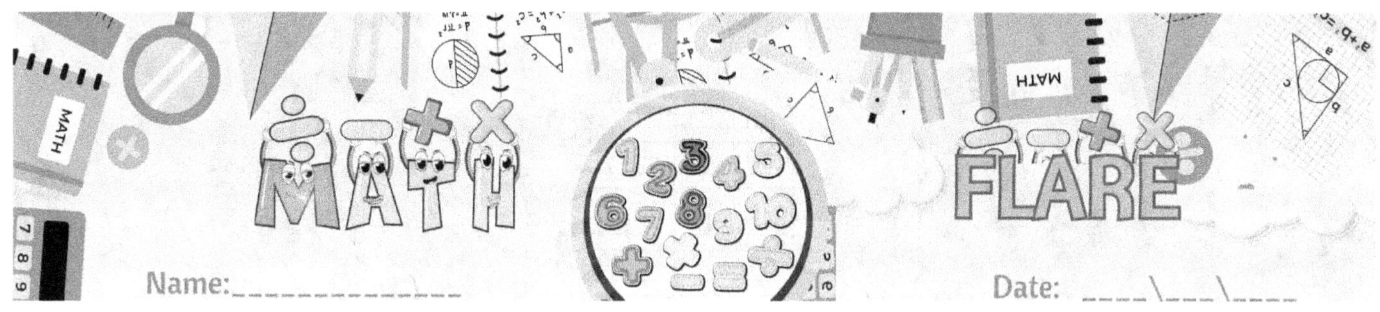

401. Alexander needs $\frac{3}{5}$ cup of flour for a recipe and he wants to make $\frac{1}{2}$ batches of the recipe, how much flour will he need in total?

402. Avery ran $\frac{4}{9}$ miles every day for 10 days. How many miles did she run in total?

403. If a recipe calls for $\frac{2}{5}$ cup of flour and you want to make it 5, how much flour do you need?

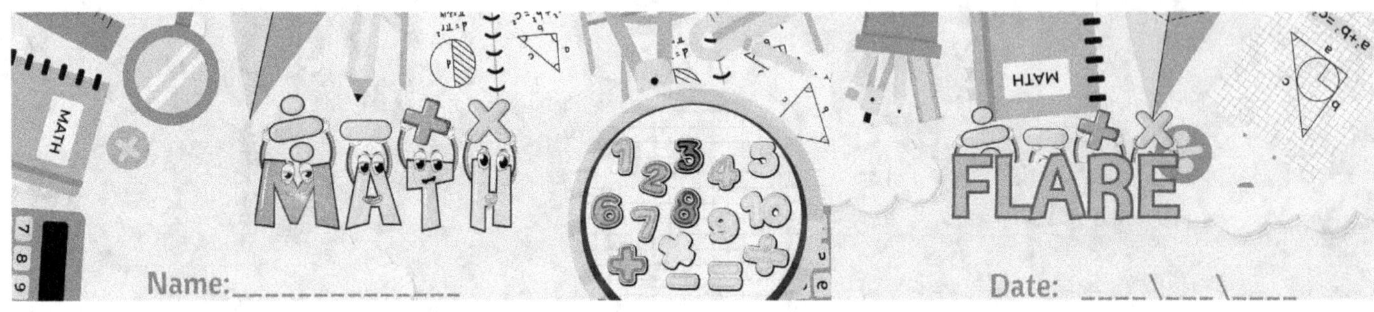

404. If a container holds $\frac{1}{2}$ of a gallon of water and you need 3 gallons of water, how many containers do you need?

405. A cake recipe calls for $\frac{1}{6}$ cups of sugar to make one cake. If Grace wants to make 6 cakes, how many cups of sugar will she need?

406. A factory can produce $\frac{4}{6}$ of a car in one hour. How many cars can the factory produce in 8 hours?

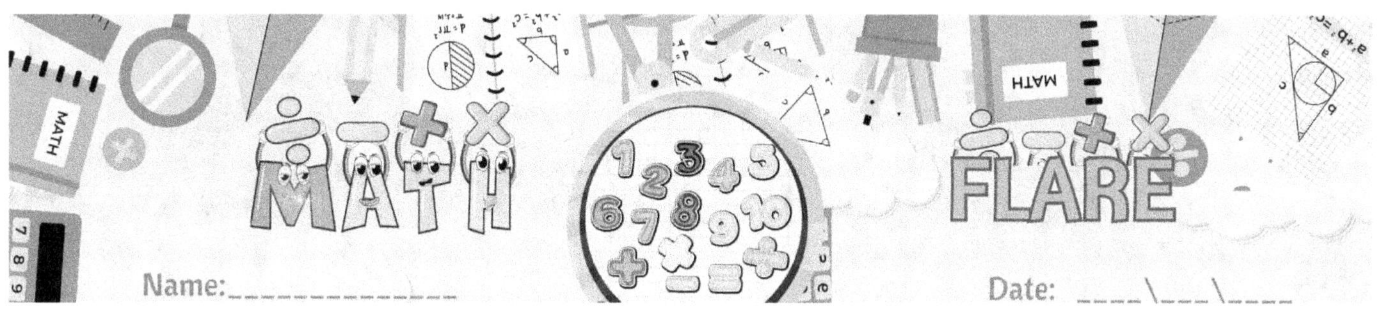

407. Tristan walked $\frac{4}{10}$ of a mile every day for 7 days. How many miles did he walk in total?

408. Nathan spent $\frac{2}{5}$ of his money to buy breads. His friend Daniel spent 3 times more to buy the breads. How much did Daniel spend?

409. If a company can produce $\frac{2}{7}$ of a product in one day, how many days will it take to produce 4 products?

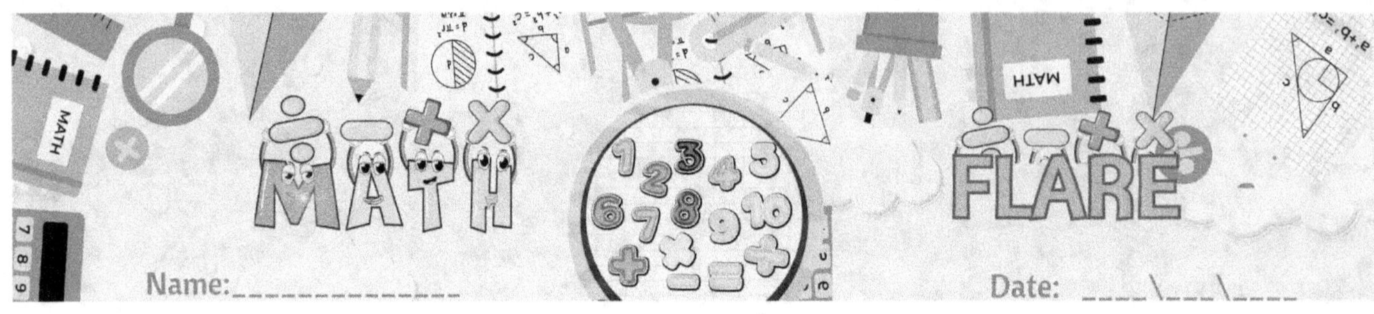

410. If a person can run at a speed of $\frac{1}{2}$ miles per hour, how long will it take him to run 4 miles?

411. If a garden has an area of $\frac{4}{7}$ square feet and you want to increase it by a factor of 2, what will be the new area of the garden?

412. A store sells $\frac{4}{5}$ of folders in one day, how many days will it take to sell 4 folders?

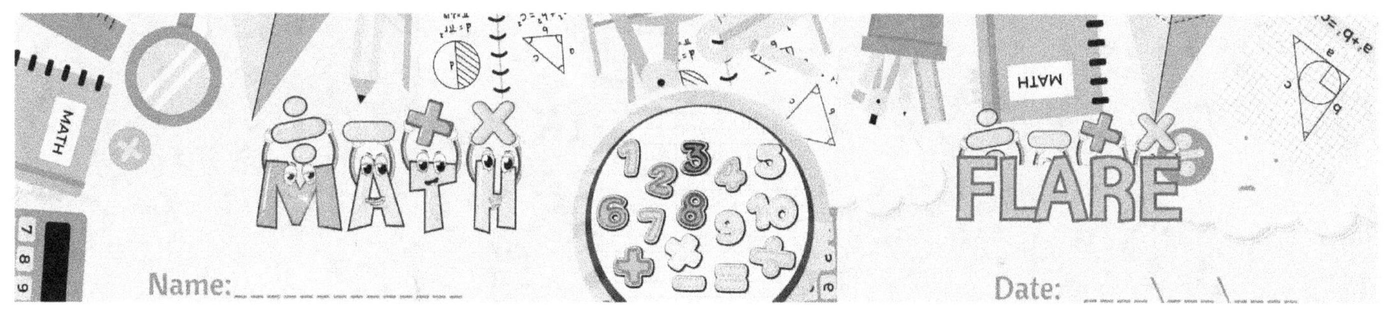

413. A school needs to make 100 cupcakes for a fundraiser. If a batch of cupcakes requires $\frac{5}{10}$ cups of sugar, how many cups of sugar will they need in total?

414. A bike tire has a radius of $\frac{2}{4}$ foot. If the tire rolls 6 times, how far does the bike travel?

415. If a car can travel $\frac{3}{5}$ of a mile on one gallon of gas, how many miles can it travel on 3 gallons of gas?

ANSWERS

Page 1:   Convert Fractions and Decimals

1. 9/20	2. 0.8	3. 0.443	4. 6/9
5. 33/40	6. 0.333	7. 0.48	8. 0.909
9. 22/36	10. 25/75	11. 0.8	12. 0.833
13. 0.333	14. 9/16	15. 948/1000	16. 1/2
17. 7/30	18. 692/1000	19. 0.333	20. 0.943
21. 10/25	22. 3/32	23. 0.067	24. 52/100
25. 0.917	26. 0.913	27. 7/19	28. 0.94
29. 44/50	30. 0.5	31. 0.786	32. 1/4
33. 8/22	34. 20/24	35. 17/18	36. 0.444
37. 47/75	38. 0.55	39. 0.6	40. 0.375
41. 0.056	42. 6/10	43. 6/7	44. 1/20
45. 1/3	46. 0.529	47. 0.333	48. 0.615

Page 5:   Mixed Numbers: Improper Fractions

49. 15/4	50. 6 25/38	51. 9 3/4	52. 17/4	53. 169/18
54. 31/12	55. 141/20	56. 15/2	57. 6 1/4	58. 91/17
59. 1 5/11	60. 28/19	61. 127/18	62. 97/16	63. 19/2
64. 39/8	65. 7/5	66. 58/11	67. 1 2/19	68. 5 1/3
69. 129/14	70. 9 1/2	71. 8 1/7	72. 8 23/26	73. 131/22
74. 69/10	75. 5 5/16	76. 5 17/20	77. 7 1/6	78. 9 7/8

79. 30/13   80. 3 5/12   81. 5/4   82. 6 6/19   83. 60/11

84. 25/7   85. 31/5   86. 39/8   87. 5 1/2   88. 23/3

89. 87/32   90. 6 1/14

Page 8: Mixed Numbers: Addition and Subtraction

91. 19/70   92. 9   93. 9 11/20   94. 9 8/21

95. 17 3/10   96. 9 5/6   97. 10 1/6   98. 22/35

99. 8 3/4   100. 4 8/9   101. 2 7/20   102. 2 29/56

103. 10 1/45   104. 6 1/3   105. 8 11/12   106. 5 23/35

107. 12 1/8   108. 4 77/90   109. 14 5/6   110. 8 7/10

111. 11/12   112. 5 11/15   113. 3 1/6   114. 19 5/56

115. 13   116. 13 5/12   117. 3 7/20   118. 19 1/10

119. 10 59/63   120. 12 1/24   121. 5 1/12   122. 11 3/10

123. 15 3/10   124. 2 1/14   125. 2 2/3   126. 9 1/30

127. 4 9/28   128. 7 13/40   129. 5 9/10   130. 3/4

131. 5/9   132. 1 5/14   133. 2 1/8   134. 5 7/12

135. 3 5/6   136. 2 9/10   137. 12 8/63   138. 7/72

Page 16: Mixed Numbers: Multiplication and Division

139. 1 13/40   140. 42 3/4   141. 10 1/8   142. 42/55

143. 125/329   144. 4 1/2   145. 32 1/2   146. 2 70/81

147. 32/33   148. 75 6/25   149. 22/27   150. 52/57

151. 3 9/133   152. 37 2/7   153. 85/88   154. 28 17/36

155. 91 5/6   156. 27/56   157. 24 2/21   158. 23 13/20

159. 6 17/28   160. 16 1/3   161. 1 1/51   162. 45/88

163. 49 3/10   164. 10 3/14   165. 36   166. 22 19/20

167. 1 19/20   168. 6 6/7   169. 8 31/36   170. 208/459

171. 112/135   172. 49 7/12   173. 1 47/93   174. 99/280

175. 3/5   176. 1 1/95   177. 79 3/4   178. 71 1/20

179. 34 5/6   180. 22 2/7   181. 3/5   182. 41 4/5

183. 20/27   184. 17 1/30   185. 37 1/8   186. 1 3/112

Page 24: Multiplication with Whole Numbers

187. 1 2/3   188. 3 1/2   189. 4   190. 3/4   191. 2 1/4

192. 3/4   193. 1/3   194. 3 9/13   195. 3 3/5   196. 5 13/19

197. 3 1/2   198. 6   199. 1/2   200. 1 11/17   201. 2 2/3

202. 1   203. 1 2/7   204. 3 3/4   205. 2 4/7   206. 7/11

207. 3   208. 2 16/17   209. 5 3/5   210. 12/13   211. 1 7/8

212. 1 3/5   213. 3 1/3   214. 2 2/3   215. 3 13/19   216. 2/5

217. 1/2   218. 2/3   219. 2/3   220. 2 1/3   221. 1

222. 2   223. 1   224. 3/16   225. 2 14/17   226. 3 7/19

227. 3   228. 5/14   229. 5 2/5   230. 2   231. 8/13

232. 4

Page 27: Simplify Fractions: Proper and Improper Fractions

233. 1/2   234. 5   235. 2/3   236. 9 1/2   237. 8

238. 8 3/4   239. 2   240. 1/4   241. 6   242. 2

243. 5/9   244. 8 1/5   245. 1/13   246. 1/4   247. 2 14/15

248. 9   249. 7/10   250. 1/3   251. 8   252. 7 1/3

253. 7   254. 7   255. 6 9/10   256. 2   257. 5

258. 2/3   259. 4 1/16   260. 5/11   261. 3 9/19   262. 3/4

263. 7   264. 9   265. 1/2   266. 7/17   267. 4 4/7

268. 1/10   269. 8 3/16   270. 2/3   271. 4   272. 4

273. 2/7   274. 3 1/2   275. 8   276. 8 7/9   277. 5 1/5

278. 10/11   279. 6 18/19   280. 2   281. 9/13   282. 6 1/2

283. 9   284. 3 1/4   285. 3 1/2   286. 2 19/20   287. 2 8/9

288. 2 3/7   289. 3 13/20   290. 7 1/3   291. 4 10/13   292. 5

293. 6   294. 9   295. 8 13/17   296. 3/4   297. 5 3/5

298. 7 16/19   299. 5/11   300. 4   301. 4/5   302. 5/14

303. 1/16   304. 3/10   305. 8   306. 3 12/17   307. 3

308. 1/4   309. 8 8/19   310. 2/7   311. 9 3/5   312. 15/16

313. 5   314. 3/11

Page 33:   Multiple Operations Fractions

315. 5 23/30   316. 8 11/42   317. 27/140   318. 31/42

319. 321/980   320. 1 1/8   321. 4/27   322. 1 11/90

323. 2 183/280   324. 7/16   325. 8 25/28   326. 6 1/6

327. 19/120   328. 13/18   329. 1 2/5   330. 11/24

331. 59/150   332. 29/84   333. 2 109/180   334. 323/756

335. 221/360   336. 7 1/9   337. 22/45   338. 7/16

339. 4 43/56   340. 1 7/20   341. 7 11/30   342. 5/8

343. 59/63   344. 2 1/3   345. 83/90   346. 2 31/210

347. 5/12   348. 18/35   349. 7/9   350. 53/90

351. 10 1/10   352. 5 10/21

Page 43: Fractions Addition Word Problems

353. 23/24   354. 9/10   355. 3/4   356. 5/6   357. 13/21

358. 17/36   359. 1/2   360. 3/4   361. 4/7   362. 37/40

363. 3/4   364. 9/14   365. 19/30   366. 8/9   367. 2/5

368. 7/12   369. 7/10   370. 5/6   371. 17/20   372. 29/36

373. 1

Page 50: Fractions Subtraction Word Problems

374. 1/20   375. 7/45   376. 19/40   377. 1/3   378. 2/9

379. 31/45   380. 3/10   381. 3/20   382. 1/15   383. 1/4

384. 1/8   385. 1/6   386. 1/4   387. 5/24   388. 5/42

389. 1/10   390. 1/9   391. 1/10   392. 7/36   393. 1/10

394. 3/40

Page 57: Fractions Multiplication Word Problems

395. 8/7   396. 1   397. 5/2   398. 14/5   399. 1/3   400. 20/3

401. 3/10   402. 40/9   403. 2   404. 3/2   405. 1   406. 16/3

407. 14/5   408. 6/5   409. 8/7   410. 2   411. 8/7   412. 16/5

413. 50   414. 3   415. 9/5

www.ingramcontent.com/pod-product-compliance
Lightning Source LLC
Chambersburg PA
CBHW081355160726
48000CB00010B/3354